Mother Mary Speaks

Beloved I Want To Tell You My Story

Mother Mary

and

Rev. Elizabeth Grace Alder

Foreword by Raymond Moody Jr., MD, PhD

Cover design by Sarah Cerulean

Cover photo by Elizabeth Alder

www.circleofmary.org

In gratitude for Her unwavering patience and
Unconditional Love, I humbly dedicate this book
to Mother Mary and to all of Her children
of which you are One.

Blessings and
Gratitude.

With Love,

from Mother Mary

and

me, Et

Contents

Foreword

Over the years, I have known people of Catholic, Protestant, Jewish and Muslim religious backgrounds who were, in their own ways inspired by Mother Mary. The deep, comforting appeal of Mother Mary across various religions for two thousand years is easy to observe and demonstrate. But to comprehend this appeal and put it in a convincing framework of rational understanding is a much harder, perhaps even an impossible thing to accomplish. That is one reason why I am drawn to this fascinating and enlightening book by my friend, Reverend Elizabeth Grace Alder.

Though not a Catholic herself, Elizabeth has experienced a personal, communicative relationship with Mother Mary for a long time. Furthermore, she has been able to extend this communicative relationship to others and build a spiritual community around Mother Mary. Her account in this book of her journey, is utterly fascinating and I feel sure that many readers will be as intrigued as I am. In fact, I suspect that Elizabeth's words and feelings will resonate in a deeply personal way.

Earlier, I mentioned that one reason I am drawn to Elizabeth's book, is that her experiences pose a challenge to the process of rational understanding. Another reason is more immediately personal. For

Mary touched me too, and my family and network of friends - incredibly, ineffably, powerfully, lovingly - a real, deep, genuine highlight of my life. And I am not even religious in any conventional sense of the word.

These events are intensely personal and involve confidences I owe to cherished other people. Besides, I don't think I could even talk about these joyous events without dissolving into tears. Suffice it to say, that the mystery of Mary continues to unfold, as it has for centuries and will continue to unfold for a long time to come.

In the meantime, I recommend Reverend Alder's book as a memorable contribution to an important, enduring spiritual tradition of humankind.

-- Raymond Moody Jr., MD, PhD, author of *Life After Life*

Introduction

I was only twenty-one when I saw Her. I stood transfixed, barely able to breathe.

The white porcelain statue of Mother Mary was simple, not ornate but beautiful. As I stood there staring up at her in the little gift shop, an unfamiliar place I had just walked in merely to look around, I felt the air become sweeter around me, so I closed my eyes to breathe it in. This was odd for me, as I had never before felt any affiliation with the mother of Jesus.

Then within my warming heart I heard Her say, "Take me home."

What? She didn't speak to me. I shook my head and said to myself, *I just imagined it. This can't be happening. Not to me!*

I took a few deep breaths and then carefully leaned forward and whispered to Mary, hoping the shopkeeper would not hear, "I'm going to walk around this little store to look around, and if I come back here again and feel this same way, I will take you home with me.*"*

I looked up at her for an answer, but her porcelain eyes were serene and unmoving as she gazed down at me. Mother Mary had captured my attention, without any effort at all, even more.

So I walked around. I think. Because I found myself standing in front of the beautiful sculpture once again, not remembering seeing anything else in the store, or if even if I had left her. Briefly, I considered walking around the shop one more time, just to make sure, but I thought, *Whatever is the point now? I'm going to take her home.* Instantly my heart was flooded with Love. My head was spinning as I looked into my small purse and found just the right amount of money to buy the statue, but no more.

Outside, the summer sun warmed my smile. Uplifted and elated, I climbed into my little blue car with my precious package. As happy as I was, I could never have realized what a special gift was awaiting me more than thirty years after this magical encounter.

From that day forward, I naturally had an altar, a sacred place in my room for Mary. Through many jobs, relationships and many moves to other cities and states, I always took Her with me. Mother Mary was the constant, the center point of my altar. I didn't say a daily prayer or perform a ritual, she was just there, lending Her quiet presence of peace in my life.

To some people who saw my altar, I needed to explain that I was not Catholic and actually, neither was She. Mary was a Jewish Mother and Jesus was

Her Jewish Son, the Messiah of His people. It was fortunate that I was raised by a Jewish stepfather and an agnostically confused mother. Not to say that all people who are agnostic are confused, my mother just had her own issues and frustrations about life in general, so she became an agnostic. This turned out to be a good thing though, because in our home we had a precious freedom, freedom of religion. Practice what you want, just don't hurt each other.

I went to a Christian church with my sister, practiced yoga, and studied Transcendental Meditation and Vedic philosophy with my brother who became a T.M. teacher. But Mother Mary loved me for some reason, and therefore Jesus was very close to my heart. My religion is kindness, healing and patience. All of these spring from the deep center of unconditional love, which Mother Mary has taken great pains and many years to teach me.

The Circle of Mary

It was 2007, exactly ten years ago as I write this, when I was getting ready for a trip to Switzerland. Oh, I was so excited! I had always wanted to see the beautiful Alps and now here was my chance to attend a convention in Murren, Switzerland with Aura Soma Color Therapy. Aura Soma is based in England and I had been studying the beautiful bottles of colors, doing healing work and giving readings from them for a few years. Since it was part of my business, I felt I could take the trip and even write it off on my taxes. Tax deduction, colors, meeting new people, as well as reconnecting with friends I had met in England, the beautiful Alps – a win, win!

On the night before the trip, I was walking from the den to the kitchen. I passed by my altar and on the way, I took a quick glance at Mother Mary. "Sit down!" she said. It was only the second time she had spoken to me (the first time, of course was in the little gift shop). Again, I wasn't sure. I doubted it even though it was as clear as a bell. So I kept going. Then, I stopped in my tracks and thought to my anxiously busy self, *Well, that could be my mind playing tricks on me, but if I don't sit down, I might miss something.*

So I went back to the altar and sat on the floor

before Her. Then almost immediately, She started talking, in my head - and fast, almost a mile a minute. "I wish to speak to the world. I urge you to let me speak to the world." I thought, *How can I do that?* Mary's answer was this, "Form a circle of women friends and call it the Circle of Mary." I was both humbled at this moment of Grace and near in disbelief that I would hear Her voice again. After I closed my mouth which I found had dropped open, I thought to myself, *Well, ok when I get back, I will get a few spiritually inclined women together, so we can sit with Mary and see what happens. Maybe after a year or so, someone will write about it. Then perhaps one day, it will be read all around the world. Certainly not me, though. I'm not a writer.* "Elizabeth," She said to make Her point clear. "This will happen all over the world."

As it was difficult to believe that Mother Mary would be talking to me, I suppose it was a blessing that I was too busy planning for my trip to truly absorb the amazement of that conversation, a direct plea from the mother of Christ.

* * *

I arrived late to the hotel in Murren, Switzerland, dizzy from jet lag and the spectacular ascent to the top of the beautiful Alps. I was completely unprepared for the scene that awaited me. Gathered in a large room, there stood a circle of nearly one hundred people, most of whom were women from over six different countries! I had been to Aura Soma courses before, in America, England, Italy and Mexico but there weren't half as many people in any of the courses I had previously attended. Mother Mary's urgency came back to me at that moment, "This will happen all over the world." With tears in my eyes I thought, *Oh Mary, how could I have ever doubted you?*

At the end of the weeklong course, I gathered names of a few women who were interested in meditating and receiving messages from Mary. I told them that I felt that we should meditate with Mother Mary for seven Sundays in a row when we got home bringing other women in a circle with them, then possibly email each other and see what comes. Seven beautiful messages did come through me and although we kept in touch, I did not hear of messages from the other women. Surprisingly to me, it seemed I was the only channel who expressed Mary's wisdom.

Here I will include two of the seven messages that were given to the Circle of Mary Sisters:

June, 2007 (The first of the messages to the Circle of Mary women.)

Dear Circle Sisters,

This beautiful morning, I meditated on Mary and visualized my sisters in the Circle around the world. I carried the white porcelain statue of Mary into the meditation labyrinth in my backyard and lovingly placed Her in the center. Sitting in front of Her with my eyes closed, I took a deep breath and felt a wonderful tranquility, surrounding me and within me.

I felt so full of peace, almost like a pregnancy and I knew that this was a feeling that only women can experience and give forth. After a few minutes, I lifted my head upwards and I sensed my spirit being transported to the outer most atmosphere of the earth. Looking down on our beautiful blue marble, I saw this fullness of peace surrounding the world.

I saw Mary, first surrounded by the color pink, then white, then lavender. She said, "These are the colors of the Peace Rainbow. Use these colors to bring peace to the world."

(Mentally and with Love, surround the Earth in these colors whenever you meditate on peace in the world.)

I know more messages will come. I encourage you to invite others to join in these important meditations of Mother Mary.

With Love,
Elizabeth

July 8, 2007

Dear Circle Sisters,

It was raining this morning (blessed rain), so I meditated on Mary inside at my altar. Since I did not feel a connection at first as I had before, I began to send the Rainbow of Peace around the world, asking that every heart be filled with this peace.

Then in a vision, I saw orbs of light falling down from the sky around me like the rain. At first, I did not understand why this was happening, I was even a little afraid and then Mary gave me the most beautiful vision of all.

She presented her Son, the Christ to me. He was in the form of a brilliant light and I thought, *How incredible it must have been to see Him walking among the crowds of people. A light so bright that all you had to do was look on Him and be healed.* I wondered why, even in His day, in His presence, that there were people who could not see that light that was so close to them. Then the room in which I sat was filled with an incredible light and I felt a peacefulness, a stillness deep within.

And then I heard the answer. "The light still shines and will always shine, but distrust and fear cause a soul to shut down, to become blind. Never be afraid to take that light for yourselves and shine it forth to the world, for this is your purpose," Mary said.

Again, I saw the orbs of light falling down

around me, and this time I pulled this light in for myself. I felt an incredible but gentle power. Fearless.

So the lesson here is: Do not be afraid of the light around you and within you. The light is there for you to claim. The light is there for you to give and help others claim it for themselves.

Expand the light. Expand peace. With love and gratefulness, Elizabeth

(Find all the messages at www.circleofmary.org.)

* * *

After the seven messages came, I began to invite women into my home for circles whenever I felt that Mary wanted them to happen. Privately, I would sit in front of Her from time to time and ask for insight. I began to write down as I "heard" her words. I was learning to hear and be confident with what She needed me to do.

In our circles, I had someone write down what Mother Mary said through me and as I didn't have a recorder at the time, the messages came so quickly that my friend just couldn't write them fast enough and some of them were lost.

Soon, it was less and less a calling of the women together and more of just myself sitting, listening and writing her messages which seemed to evolve over time. Mary was a patient teacher.

Sometimes I had a specific question. At other times I would just sit, listen and write the message or lesson that she gave.

Then on April 12, 2016, Mother Mary asked me to do something she had not asked me to do before.

Beloved,

I Want to Tell You My Story

I sat down to meditate with Mary, seeking relief from a busy day, to relax and bask in Her perfect peace. The sun was just going down, flickering its last light across the altar. It was evening time and there were no distractions, so I opened my heart to hers and I thought, *Mother Mary, is there anything you want to tell me on this beautiful night?*

A moment later she said, "Beloved, I want to tell you my story." The words within my heart from Mother Mary were more clear and concise than I had ever received before.

What?! Sitting straight up, I looked around the empty room. *Are you speaking to me?* I began to shake my head as I said to Her, "Oh no! No Mother Mary, not me! Oh please, I cannot. I am not, not worthy!" Tears fell from my eyes and I began to cry in jagged sobs.

"Elizabeth, write!" she said.

And thus, Mary and Her reluctant writer began.

* * *

Before I was born, in the womb of my mother, I knew of my purpose. Of course, my father wanted a son, strong of body, mind and Spirit. But my dear Mother, knew I was a girl and she felt doubly blessed. As her belly grew, a Light was shown within her. People would exclaim, "Anna what is this Light that you carry?"

Within her womb, I heard all. And I knew it was the Light of God pouring through me, through my growing body, becoming ready for the world.

Now the Soul knows these things, but at the moment of the trauma of birth, and this is the plan of God, there is the forgetting. We forget so that there is a clean slate, so to speak. There is a new period of learning, a focus on the present incarnational time, time to start anew.

In a new incarnation, a new life, there is not the time to relive the past. Each lifetime's lessons, each single day is packed full, as you would call it.

Even the days when it would seem to you that there is nothing going on, nothing happening. These days are carefully fitted into the lifetime for a reason, for a purpose.

Yet at the moment I was born, because God had such a plan, I knew of my purpose. I did not know or understand the physical ramifications, the unfoldment of what was yet to come, whom I would meet, or what path I would follow.

However, I knew and felt within every bone of

my body, every breath that I took, that God's constant, eternal Love was expressed within my being. That I was an instrument for Him, a Holy One to channel this Love to Humanity. This I knew.

There was no choice, you see. There was no, "Yes I will, or No I will not," for the Presence of God's Love flooded my entire Life, my Being. And yet my heart felt great compassion for those of this world.

* * *

At times my mother had to force me to eat, as I felt no need for food. "You must eat, my Mary," she would say as she put the beans, grapes, olives and fish before me. "You need your strength, for the strong are the most devoted." She said things such as these in her coaxing.

My father was a kind man but spoke few words. He let my mother and me do all of the talking. We would laugh and play together, my mother, Anna, and I. And it seemed that whenever I spoke, my father would grow even more quiet, as if to absorb, like a thirsty cloth, the words that I was speaking. He was a listener and therein was his gift.

Never did I know fear as a child. I felt and saw Angels constantly by my side, beautiful incandescent Beings of Light, and I knew they were there to protect me. I was an only child, but I did not feel alone.

Our home was small at first, made out of mud from the sand with palm leaves on the roof for protection and cooling from the hot sun in the day; but through the years my father, with the help of friends in our community, added rooms to increase our comfort. As my father's grapevines and olive trees grew, so did our home. The prayer room was my favorite and when I was not being taught at the temple, or helping my mother, it was there that I found my retreat.

As I grew and my body changed, my mother, following God's guidance, separated me from the men in our family and in our village more and more and for longer lengths of time, as we went into a cave dwelling in the hills. Weeks went by, then months and then years. I truly missed my kind, quiet father, whom it seemed, could never stop working.

He had a new grove of olive trees, grapevines, donkeys and cattle to attend. If a neighbor was in need of help, he was always there to lend a strong hand. I learned earthly love and quiet strength from my father.

In our place of retreat, tucked inside the hills, we would sit, read and study scriptures together in the morning and at night. I could never get enough! The stories about God's words made my heartfelt love for Him ever stronger. I would often protest when Mother put the scrolls away. Our paper was not so strong as yours, and she would say, "Mary we must prepare our meal now. These precious papers will fall apart from your so much touching them!" My mother would laugh even as she said this sternly. I learned both laughter and devotion from my dear mother.

Of course, I soon knew the written words by heart, but I also knew that these inscriptions were Holy and I wanted to feel and touch and be in their presence. "Oh bless the devoted ones!" I would exclaim. "Who listened to God's words and diligently wrote them down, that I might read and hold them in my hands!"

We were isolated; however, travelers would stop by occasionally. In some way, they would say they knew when to bring us food and things that we needed. However, I had very little contact with them. My mother forbade me to speak when they came, for when I did by happenstance, they would always ask to stay a little longer, and they would protest when she politely asked them to leave so that we might continue our prayers. They said it was my voice that gave them peace within their souls.

If the travelers came with children, it was to them that I was allowed to talk. "The child which you will one day bring into the world, will be the Voice of Peace," my mother would say, "and you will ascend because of Him." Of these words, I paid little attention, not because I doubted her, but because I was young and even the most devoted in their youth do not always understand the words of the wise. Even so, I knew she was wise and truly guided by our God. She always knew what to say at the right time. I never defied her and I followed her authority completely.

Hardly a week would go by when we did not hear from my dear father. Traveling friends from our tribe brought his precious messages to us in small earthen jars. We eagerly received them and pulled the scrolled paper out gently. It was difficult, sometimes, to wait until our visitors would leave so that we could read them aloud together. The messages were always filled with love. *I miss you my dear ones! May God be with you always as I hold you in my prayers, morning and night*, He would write.

My father would sometimes include news of our family tribe as well and let us know who might need the attention of our prayers.

My mother would send her loving writings and prayers in return. Exchanging the little brown jars, she would also inform him of how I was growing strong in body, mind, and above all in Spirit, ever closer to God. Some of the jars she kept, for these were special gifts from my father, filled with rose petals and aromatic herbs from his garden. Enclosed might be a note saying, *A reminder of God's blessing from the earth, as well as, my deep love for you, dear Anna.* I knew this to be a joy and a comfort to her.

The Consummation

One warm night, the Angels woke me from a deep sleep. "Wake up! Wake up! Rise, oh blessed One!" they sang. "For God is calling you."

(Here dear reader, I said to Mary, "Oh wait, this must be your most intimate, sacred moment of conception. I should not write about this!" "Write Elizabeth!" she said. "For it was no shadow that came over me, as is written in your Bible, but a beautiful, blissful Light. Write!" So I bowed my head again in humble, tearful gratitude and listened).

From the shore, the sea, the waters of Galilee, I heard God's whispers calling me. "Mary, arise!" In full obedience, I quickly walked from our hidden cave to the shore, the stars and the moon brightly lighting my way. Facing the waves and the wind, I stood still and the breath of God came over me, as fragrant as the most fragrant rose of the heavens. Soon I was filled with His Holy light, so that no part of myself was then of human form.

Dear reader, as you now pause to close your eyes and feel the peace within you, know that this would be just a minute knowledge of my consummation. I was transformed as a Being of Light. It was such a feeling of heavenly bliss, not of this world, and there was no room for fear within me. Every breath, every part of myself was filled with Divine Love as I surrendered, completely and fully into the Illuminance.

It was the darkest of the night's hour and yet, the shore and waters were bathed in a beautiful, brilliant Light. The birds woke singing from their slumber and the sea's waves greatly swelled as the fish leapt out of the water as if filled with great joy! I was One with the Beloved, the Highest and the Holiest of All.

It seemed that time, the most elusive measurement of all, ran quickly and slowed down all at once. Then a great peace came around me; my heart was filled and poured forth the Love of God, unconditional, strong, and yet almost unbearable in its perfection. I fell to the ground praising His name, asking and knowing that this Light, this Enlightenment, would never leave me.

Yes, I was crying also. I was crying for joy, weeping for the gratitude of this Blessing, of God's Holy Love, which had come to me alone. Then, there on the sand, I closed my eyes and almost in an instant slipped into the sweetness of a deep sleep, the protective Love of God and the Holy Host of Angels singing softly to my heart.

I awoke in the early morning on the golden, sandy shore, when the first light of dawn brushed my eyes. I stood up and my heart knew that there was no doubt that God had planted a growing seed within me. I felt an exquisite fullness of Love and I was uplifted in sweet gladness. It was then that I knew it was time for me to marry, to go back home to our village.

I awoke my sleeping mother and told her it was time now for me to take a husband. My mother agreed immediately, as if she knew this moment was coming. She confessed then that she and my father had been praying for God to send a good, devout man who would be chosen for me to marry.

Although we were miles away from Jerusalem, I being kept away from our village, my parents, of course, at times communicated by messengers, but they had also communicated through their dreams. They had such great love for one another, they truly knew each other by heart. My mother, Anna, told me that a husband had recently been chosen for me and that seven days before this morning, she had received a message from my father. He had had a dream that I was finally ready to meet my betrothed one.

Home

It was a hot day when we left our cave hut in the hills. I could hear the waves crashing against the shores of Galilee, which seemed to be speaking my name, reminding me of the night of my consummation, my enlightenment, the breath of roses opening my heart. "Make haste!" my mother laughed as she prodded the donkey forward. I was riding our donkey and she followed, walking at the start. Each hour or so, we took our turns on our patient beast.

My mother was a strong woman with long, black hair and brown eyes, which always had a twinkle of sweet joy. Her skin was golden in the sun. When it was agreed that it was our time of leaving, she arose without hesitation. Our packing – the small loom, the food, the little message urns, our clothing and bedding – was done almost in an instant. I understood, then, that this time had been expected all along. Of course, our Holy Scripture writings took a little more time to pack and put away safely. "Careful, careful!" my mother and I said together as we lovingly rolled them up and placed them in the wooden box, which was placed on top of all our belongings.

Before the first step of our journey home, we knelt together in prayer, thanking our Father in

Heaven for all that He had given us and for our blessings yet to come. Then we said a prayer, also, for our kind donkey, for strength and gratitude in bringing us home.

I tell you this part of my story, of the road to our home, because it was so significant and it was in fact, surprising to my mother and me. The Angels helped us along the way, of course. A journey, which would have usually been difficult and tiring, was fast and easy for us. It seemed that day as if time was nothing. We were happy and singing praises to the Lord. I remember feeling so alive and wonderful and my mother laughed at how I was beaming. "It is good to feel joy in the Lord's Grace!" she would say.

So many people came to help us along the way as we traveled. We started out carrying our burdens with one donkey and then we had three! Delicious food, figs, grapes and olives were offered and cooked fish, fresh from the sea, as well. "My cup runneth over," my beautiful mother's voice sang. "Surely goodness and mercy will follow me all the days of my life," I sang in happy return. The kind-hearted travelers sang with us, bringing us much more than we needed. "We are truly headed home." I heard my mother say to herself in a whisper. She had missed my father and could barely contain the happiness of returning.

Our hearts were truly bursting with joy as we

finally passed the Temple wherein I had spent much of my childhood days. I could hear the prayers rising in volume within as we drew closer.

Every evening, as the last of the daylight drew nigh, the men of our tribe would go into the temple and pray in gratitude and praise of the Holy Father after working long days. This was a ritual that my father would never miss. Even so, I am sure he felt the presence of my mother close by, though he could not see her; because it was his voice, I knew, that I heard praying a bit more loudly at first, and then the other voices followed along. Thus was the closeness of their hearts. I, Mary, was their only child, and even though I delighted in the Lord and His Loving Wisdom, I felt within myself a longing for a companion now. A husband who would be my faithful protector, provider, and friend. Until now, I had needed nothing more than God and my parents' love. I had friends and beloved teachers along the way, but God was always, always first and foremost in my heart. What here was this stirring within?

An Angel's whisper touched me at that moment, the moment when we entered my childhood home. "Fear not, favored daughter of the Most High. The longing you feel was placed in your heart by God Himself. Soon, that which you seek will be presented unto you." And I was comforted and glad again.

What was coming into my life was, as you

know, the greatest gift of my life and of the world, and also, the hardest. But of course, this was not given for me to see at that time. For God in His Grace casts a veil over our eyes, ears and hearts so that we might taste just a small morsel that is on our plate at a time.

What wisdom and kindness there is, in this His Plan! What a wonderful, harmonious life everyone in the world would enjoy if everyone would savor each morsel, whether bitter or sweet, knowing it was the offering from God's Hands, from His own plate, His gift! We would never spit it out in anger, disappointment, or disrespect – thinking we had somehow made it ourselves, or that it had been handed to us by a random mistake.

Every bite of Life is precious. A gift from God to be savored, touched, tasted, smelled, heard, and admired with reverence. All life, all light, is emanating from the Heart of the Holy One.

* * *

The sun was quickly sinking as we arrived home and after drinking some milk, I felt tired and went straight to my bed. I heard my father come in and I wanted just to listen to his voice, but I fell asleep in mid-prayer. It had been a long journey and a very long time since I had been home. "Sleep, blessed Mary," the Angels sang softly to my heart. "Sleep now, the beautiful morning comes soon."

In the morning, I awoke to my parents' hushed, but excited talking about the dreams they had had through the night. Groggy from slumber and respectfully not listening too closely, I heard such things as, "An Angel bowed down before me!" and "What is this new light?"

I felt surrounded, verily wrapped up in the unbounded Love of my parents' hearts and even more so in the Great Love of God. If my feet touched the ground when I went in to greet my father for the first time in over three years, I can scarce remember. I hugged him so tightly that he exclaimed, "Oh my loving daughter! I cannot breathe! Let go and tell me about your years away from me!" I held him a little longer and then told him and my mother about the Light of God which had come upon me. In that moment, we all knelt down in reverence and in prayer.

The weeks that followed were a preparation and many hours spent at the loom, making a new and special garment for me. "It is now that you will need a new cloth to wear," my dear mother told me. "For your father has found for you a husband."

"As you have said, my Mary, it is time for you to marry. His name is Joseph. He is a devout man. A good carpenter from a good family also, from the house of David. He will be strong and he will build for you a good and loving home."

As soon as she began to speak of him, saying

his name was Joseph, I felt a rush of love in my heart that I had never known before, and I already knew he was to be sent to me by God. "Yes! I said. "I agree with my whole heart that he is the one I shall marry, my dear mother, Anna, for God has touched my heart just now!"

The Nativity

"It won't be long now, my Joseph," I remember saying. "No, Mary, I know it, too," my husband whispered, as he tried to cool my face with a cloth. "Not long, not long."

"The innkeeper's wife has been so kind. Please, would you go and get her now?" I knew God and His Angels were close, that I was giving birth to His child, but here in Bethlehem, away from my childhood home, all I could think of was the overwhelming pain that gripped my body.

I suffered in labor as every woman had suffered before me and would after. The innkeeper's wife had brought extra blankets and strips of cloth. She told us that she would return shortly to the stable corner, which she had made clean for me as best she could. Her name was Rachel and she had told us that she had helped many babies come into this world.

I lay on the ground with hay and a blanket underneath. Blankets covered me as well. It was a cold night, but I felt so hot. Sweat poured from my face. I wanted so to throw off the blankets, but there was little privacy and no door to shut tight. I longed greatly for my mother's loving touch and I cried out for her. Rachel then appeared with a knowing smile, and I was calm again. My worried husband stepped back while Rachel knelt before me and exclaimed, "Push, oh blessed daughter, for the child of the world is coming now!"

Within me, I felt a seizing, terrible pain and a blissfulness beyond words both at once, and then indeed the child of God came forth. He cried only once, but it seemed like a song! A Voice from the Heavens.

And at that moment, there was complete silence in the stalls. There was stillness. No animal, no creature moved at all. The sounds from the inn, a short walk behind us, seemed to cease as well. It was as if the entire Universe took in its breath and held it still. This is what my husband has told me.

Yet, all that I could notice, was the Light in my baby's face, his loving eyes and the pure joy I felt as I looked on him and held him close. For just a few tender moments, He was mine only and I said a silent prayer of gratitude for this gift that God had granted me, His humble servant. A promise from the Angels! Tears of joy and release streamed down my face and wet my baby's head, as he nestled closer and took all that I could give him.

"His name is Jesus," my husband said as he slowly knelt closer to us. "The Angel did tell me that this would be his name." Joseph's eyes were wet as well and shining with love. He bowed his head in prayer. "Lord, thank you for allowing me to be ever your servant, the protector of your Son and

His beautiful mother." Then looking into my eyes with a sweetness I had not seen before, he took my hand and said, "It is only the Lord God that I love more in this world, my Mary. I will always be with you and I will raise your son as my own." "Yes," I nodded, my heart full of love, for I could not yet speak.

Dear Rachel came forth to clean us, the baby and me, with water and milk from her cow who had followed in near. The innkeeper's wife had brought in no lamp, but it seemed our tiny stable was now made warm and brightly lit. Soon, other animals came close in to see the child as well. My heart, mind, and soul were in wonder, and even though others from the inn and the fields came to gather about, to see our son and to tell us of the Brilliant Star, I felt peaceful and protected by God's Holy Host of Angels. Of course, we knew that there was no need of fear or anxiousness. All would be provided, for this was His Holy Plan.

Joseph helped me up and, as it was written, we wrapped the Christ child up in swaddling clothes to keep Him warm and placed Him in the manger, so that those who came in would be able to see Him better. He was not just our son, this we knew. He was God's Loving gift to all beings of the world. We could barely look away at the sight of this incredible child, this light of Love, who was given in our care. Even so, I was amazed at the continuous stream of villagers and shepherds from the hills beyond, who came to see our son on the night of His birth. My Joseph was, of course, protective and only let them get close enough to see for a moment and then, thanking them, led them away.

Each person, I could tell in their eyes, had an immediate change. At first, I expect, they were curious. They had heard the news of a wondrous event that had happened in little Bethlehem and wanted to see if it was true. But when they looked upon Him, when they saw the radiance of God's Light, their eyes transformed to utter Love and truly, each one fell upon their knees. They said such things as: "Glory to God in the Highest!" "The Messiah of Peace has finally come!" and "I will not give harm to my family or anyone ever again!" To those who repented such as this, Joseph, in his kindness, let them stay a little longer as they wept. Even three great men, breathing heavily from traveling fast on their camels and bearing precious gifts, came from far away. "We came to help Herod," they said upon leaving. "But now, seeing the child, the Glory of God, we will protect Him always from harm."

After a few hours, the visitors stopped coming and then the Angels covered us in a blanket of sweet peace so that we could take our rest. It was then that I knew that the communication between my infant son and I was immediate and immeasurable. I had no other to teach me what to do as a new mother, how to take care of a baby; so Jesus was my teacher from the start.

No, He did not speak to me in words, of course, but even without fussing or crying, He let me know His needs and almost immediately, I knew; I had no need to question. He was so patient with me. If I was tired or did wrap Him up wrongly, He would wait a little while and make just the slightest sound until I understood.

* * *

Joseph, my husband, was an Earth Angel, as you would say. The day we were introduced by our parents we both knew that it was God's Holy Plan that we would be together all of our lives. Joseph was my strong protector, my gentle guide and my antenna, always alert to that which might be coming. I trusted his steadfastness completely. When I say to you that he was my antenna, I am speaking of his dreams.

Joseph was truly a devout man. On the first day we said our prayers together, my heart leapt for joy, for I knew that his love and trust in the Lord God matched mine.

From his linage, the House of David, the men knew that dreams were true messages from God. It is unfortunate that men from many tribes have lost this ability.

This sacred ability has been lost because of

greed, in the thinking that they must be in control and not God. We weep in sadness for their loss.

One of the first things Joseph said to me was this, "Mary, I have had many dreams of your light." He did not mean to say this in a romantic way, he meant it truly. God had chosen him for me and from his childhood, he had had messages, Divine instructions on how to live his life, to prepare for the responsibility of raising the child of the Most High. Joseph was raised by his good parents to pay great attention to his dreams and not forget them.

Know this in truth, God did not randomly choose my husband. Joseph knew his role as I did, from the beginning of his life.

Through his dreams, Joseph faithfully guided and protected Jesus and myself. He woke me up in the early morning before the sun rose to rise as he packed up our belongings. "Quick!" "Quick as you can, dear Mary! We must arise now and leave, for I have dreamed it!"

I bundled up the baby and with a fast breakfast and prayer with Rachel, we let her know that we were setting off for the land of Egypt. Herod, my husband was told, meant to kill us and our child, so we could not stay in Bethlehem a moment longer.

My heart was full as we journeyed on. In this time, I felt every emotion, familiar and unfamiliar to me, that seemed possible. I was overjoyed with the newness of motherhood, magnified by the knowledge that my son was the true Son of God. In knowing this, I felt secure, peaceful and protected. I also felt so humbled that the Lord would have chosen me and my dear Joseph to raise such a child as He.

I felt uplifted and light as I looked ahead at the rising sun. Incredibly, only one day later, my body was completely healed from giving birth. I had helped other women in my tribe and knew of the slow recovery, the pain and exhaustion of birthing, sometimes for weeks after their children were born. Therefore, I knew this to be a miracle, but I kept it to myself. All I said to Joseph when he asked how I was feeling, if we should stop awhile to rest was, "I am fine, my husband. God's Love does keep me strong." And indeed, it was truth. I had all the energy I needed to travel with my new baby.

A Hidden Homecoming

The journey was very unlike the homebound journey I took with my mother. It was in secret that we left, hiding the light we carried, away from the eyes of strangers who might question us, or do Him harm. And even though I felt the protective presence of the Angels, through Joseph's telling dream and my natural instinct as a mother, I held my baby close, hidden by a blanket so no one else could see.

Of course, He was as peaceful and quiet as only He could be. Stirring gently against my body whenever it was time to nurse and be kissed and held even closer. The slow, easy walking of my faithful donkey took care of the swaying and the rocking of our son. I whispered the lullabies of the Angels, praising the Lord in every song, so that no one else could hear.

Joseph and I had told the innkeeper's wife that we would be traveling to Egypt. We knew she might be asked of our whereabouts. We did not tell her, however, that first we would travel to Jerusalem, and then later continue our journey to Egypt. According to the Laws of our faith, we needed first to take our son to the home of my parents and take our shelter there.

Oh, my mother, Anna, was so happy to see us!

My father, Josiah, was as well, but due to our secrecy, all greetings were subdued. We ate, rested, and shared our stories in hushed tones. "We heard about the beautiful star in Bethlehem. The brightest! And the singing of the Angels, Glorifying God, heard by everyone," said my mother, leaning toward me in a whisper. "We knew, your father and I, and our hearts were overjoyed. But we kept these things only to ourselves, holding you, the baby and Joseph in our prayers and hearts."

My infant son took hold of Anna's outstretched finger as she leaned closer toward her grandson. "My Mary, I am humbled in the presence of you and your Blessed Child." Her sweet brown eyes twinkled as she looked down at him and I was overwhelmed by the tears of Love from my mother and for the gift of Love from God, who had blessed me among women.

As was the custom of our Jewish tribe, devout and following the Laws of Moses, my baby and I stayed in a separate part of the house during my days of purification. I was already healed from the birthing, and as I have told you, I kept this miracle of healing to myself, only sharing it with my mother. We were separated from the men and felt the blessing of it.

This is not to say that we did not have love for my father and my husband, nor did they mistreat us in anyway. They were kind and benevolent kings in our eyes, always loving and attentive and good company as well. But our Law of faith was that after the birth of a child, the women would be separated for nearly forty days.

For this we were glad. It was time for my mother and I to be alone together, to share wisdom, to be peaceful. It was time for ourselves. It was a time to gather our strength and also a time for our men to miss our daily presence. Our families would draw even closer after these days of separation.

My father, giving homage to his new grandson, allowed that we stay, my mother and I, in the rooms of my parents. There was more light, more space, in this room, and it was cooler during the heat of the day, and also away from the heat of the cooking.

My mother's constant presence made my heart feel doubly blessed, and I was reminded of my days spent alone with her in the caves of hills. I realized, at last, that she had been guided, even before I was born, by the Highest of Angels to prepare me for this time. Time to bear God's son and to nurture Him.

Each day with my new son was more glorious than the last. I knew that with the guidance of the Angels and my mother's attentive presence that we would help to prepare Him for His sacred time here on Earth. I would look into His Loving eyes, full of light, full of knowing, and find a peace I could not put into words. Never did He cry aloud, for I knew every need He may have had, and He seemed to know as well that our presence in Nazareth could not be known.

On the eighth day of His birth, my mother brought my baby son to the men for His circumcision. The ceremony was performed in the prayer room of the house. Anna told me that my husband, father and uncle were there to attend with the eldest Rabbi of our tribe. "Oh my, Mary," she later told me, "as I walked in, when they took sight of your baby, each man fell on his knees and were overcome with tears. For they knew that they would be holding and performing this rite for the Son of God." Blessed are we, Mary, for we are in the Presence of the Lord made flesh!"

The hour of praying and singing to God and readings of the Holy Scriptures before the procedure were kept as quiet as possible. I could smell the burnt offering, which was small because of our circumstance. I felt the great devotion of the prayers and songs to God, which were both more muted and fervent than ever before.

I stood behind the closed door of the room of separation and listened closely to every sound. Truly, I was listening most intently for the sound of my child's cry.

A child's cry during the circumcision ceremony was familiar to me. I had spent much time in the Temple where baby boys of our extended family and tribe had felt this pain and cried long and loudly. Therefore, my heart was beating fast and my tears were already falling, stinging my eyes and face. My mother had given me a wet cloth to wring in my hands and to hold to my mouth. I waited to hear the cries and held my breath at the last prayer. But, there was no crying and I heard the men draw in their breath as they saw this, His Acceptance.

A quiet stillness, a pause followed. It was time to name the child of God. Then I heard Joseph's low voice. "In a dream, the Angel of God gave me His name. Jesus." Each man and then my mother spoke the name. "Jesus, Jesus, Jesus, Jesus, Jesus." I said it, too, finally able to say the name Joseph and I already knew. "Jesus."

As I spoke the word, "Jesus," a breath of Holy Reverence filled the room and I heard a whispering in my ear. "Yes, Jesus, my Son," and I fell to my knees in gratitude and praised God in whispered tears, again and again.

Soon my husband slowly opened the door and brought my son to me. Joseph's eyes, brown with flecks of gold, were shining with love. He was a big man, tall and strong of body. He was a crafter of great buildings, and yet he held Jesus in his arms with great care and tenderness. He did not speak, as not one soul in the house had words that were sufficient at this time of such Grace. I took our now named son, Jesus, into my arms and smiled a "thank you" to my husband as he closed the door that he, himself, had made.

My mother brought in the food of the celebration for me. The smallest of celebrations, as God had shown us, can be the most profound. I started to protest. "Dear mother, Anna, I am not hungry. God has filled me this night and I shall fast!" Of course, she looked at me and smiled knowingly. "God has blessed you among women, my Mary; eat and be a strong, nourishing mother for His Son. Now, allow me to hold Him while you eat this meal, which I have prepared and God has blessed."

Thus, handing my sleeping son to my mother, I sat on the eating mat and gave thanks for the food before me. It was the most delicious meal I had ever tasted! The grapes from the vines and the olives from my father's trees were better than I had remembered, even though I had eaten them all of my life. The fish – baked in Palm leaves – was a recipe my mother had always made during special festivities, but this night it excelled all expectations.

I was praising God with every morsel I put in my mouth. It was almost as if my taste senses had just come alive after a deep sleep. I turned to look at my mother as she sat cooing and holding God's Son. My eyes were wide with wonder as I thought, *What miracle is this, that food is more than just a nourishment?*

"Yes," she said, lifting her face and beaming. "Already."

* * *

I had more than thirty days and nights after the ceremony to spend alone with my son and my mother. It was blessed, sweet, devotional and magical. The words I express here barely touch the feelings I knew in this time, and the time went by too quickly.

As I have said concerning time, when we feel that nothing is happening, so much growth of Spirit is happening within. In the hours and days alone, I would lie and sleep, nurse, and talk to my son, and I could feel Him growing right beside me. I took in all of the delicious food my mother brought to me. She had prayed over the food as it was being prepared, and of course, I said my prayers of gratitude as well. My body grew fat and strong along with the Holy child. We were growing together, becoming ready for the journey into Egypt.

"Please bring me the family Holy writings, my Mother," I had asked early on. "You already know them by heart, my daughter. Why don't you recite them to your son?"

"Oh, but I love the feel of them, the smell of them, as I read from the scriptures. The Holy presence is so close when I hold them in my hands!

And I know Jesus would love to touch them, too!"

"But Mary," my mother began to protest, "He is but a few weeks old and His little hands will crumple and soil the pa--." She stopped in mid-sentence, in the middle of her word. Anna put her hands over her heart and laughed with a tear running down her cheek. Then she leaned close and brushed His soft, dark hair with her fingers. "Yes, little One, I will grant your wish."

Within the hour, all of our family's writings and scriptures were brought into the room with reverence. My mother laid the wooden box on the bed in silence and left the room quietly, as Jesus was sleeping comfortably by my side. She gave me a knowing smile, and for the first time in my life, she did not ask me to be very careful with its contents.

I arose and carefully moved the box and its papers onto the floor and sat beside it. As I touched the Holy Scripture and the history of my family, I could hear the whisperings, the teachings of God's Angels close to my ears and my heart. These whisperings were inaudible to others, except for my son, who stirred and smiled calmly in His sleep.

The scriptures bring knowledge – rich and vast – but at times needs the Angel's help in the interpretation. For many of these stories were written in code and hold many beautiful layers of teachings. Be careful, dear reader, to go within and ask for guidance while reading the scriptures, so that it is the Angels, the Highest Source, who will reveal their meaning to you and not the human ego, which can be self-serving, and therefore blinded to the Truth.

So here, dear reader, is how best to read the Holy Scriptures in order to receive the full meaning, the depth of their Wisdom.

As you hold them in your hands, in whatever form they may be, close your eyes for a moment and know that this for you, is a sacred time. Then pray that you would receive the blessing, the knowledge from these writings, that which is right for you to know. Turn towards the Wisdom of God and you will always be served truly.

Eager to read from the Holy Scriptures again, I gently lifted the scrolls from the box. Jesus opened His sweet, slumber-filled eyes and even the birds outside fell silent as I spoke the words of the sacred writings, the history and Laws of our people.

This privilege, the reading of the Scriptures, was normally given only to the men of the family, but of course, my situation was blessedly exceptional. I was an only child and now the mother of the Son of God Himself. This knowledge weighed both light and heavy on my shoulders. At times I could barely breathe with the thought of it. Not for fear or pride, but for the humble gratefulness, of this Holy Gift from God.

Within this box, also, were papers I had not seen before. There was a drawing, done by my father of a house similar to ours in the beginning, before other rooms had been added to. I held with awe a letter written of the marriage commitment between my parents. Both my mother and my father wrote the first letters of their names upon it, J and then A. At the bottom of the paper, I could barely make out the name of our Rabbi, who would soon receive my son at the Temple.

My father could draw quite well it seemed, but was so busy working and helping others as they needed, he had not the time to develop this skill, as did other artists within our community. I would like to add that it was also forbidden, in that time, to draw a likeness of the women of our tribe.

However, because of rules such as these and the inability of many of our tribe, who neither could read nor write, the minds of our people were quick and sharp. It was considered a great skill to cultivate then, to tell a long story from beginning to end, an accurate memory of things that had occurred even very long ago. Perhaps to the beginning of time when God blessed the Earth and shone His Light upon it.

* * *

It was the day after my time of separation, and Joseph and I packed up as few possessions as possible that very night. Then we went into the prayer room with our child and said our evening prayers together for the first time in many weeks. I had missed him. It was a solemn time for us both, and yet we were both glad to be together again. As we held our hands tightly together, we prayed for strength, protection and guidance of our Loving God, to bring us through the coming journey to Egypt, a land that we had never seen. Even though I knew this was God's protective plan for us, I did not want to leave. Joseph, of course, felt compassion for my longing to stay, but he had had the dream again and was ready to do the bidding of the Lord.

Lifting my bowed head with his great hands, he saw the tears running down my cheeks as I held Jesus close and said, "Mary, be comforted! For deep in my heart, I know that God will return us to Nazareth and to your parents. As God's grateful servant, I will ever be by your side, protecting and loving you and the Holy child." Smiling at Joseph, I fell in love with my husband, chosen for me by God, even more in the prayer room of my childhood home.

* * *

The morning air was cold as we arose to walk to the Temple. The sun would not rise over the hills for yet another hour. My thoughts seemed to be in many places at once during the walk into city of Jerusalem. This was the day we would present Jesus at the Holy Temple, as this was the Law of our people, the Law of Moses. It was the time of our purification, my son and mine. I was proud and full of love. I was filled with the love of a mother and overflowing with the Love of God's blessing on this sacred day.

I confess, though, that I had felt within me a sadness and a hesitation, as I knew this was indeed the day we would flee to Egypt, leaving my parents and the comfort of their loving home far behind.

That sadness was small compared to the knowing of my husband's dream. That we were in a hurry to take little Jesus, to protect Him from the sword of Herod, who sought to kill Him. However, we had no fear as we approached the Temple square, for above and around it there were so many Angels that I could not take count. The sun was just beginning to touch the horizon when we arrived and yet the Temple seemed to be ablaze with Holy Light.

My mother saw this too, and spoke softly into my ear, "Oh, I can see the Heavenly Host of Angels, my Mary, and I will worry no more about you and your little One! All is in the favor of the Lord."

My family and I were in awe and wonder as we approached the arched entryway. Simeon, an elderly man whom we knew from our tribe, came up first to greet us. "Please, dear one, may I hold the child?" he said with a quiet urgency. And to my surprise, I placed Jesus in his arms without question. Then said he, "Oh, Holiest of Holy, you have greatly blessed me this day. My Lord, you have brought your promise unto me!" Then he looked down at Jesus's face. "Master, I have waited for this day. At long last, You have come and now I am allowed to go in peace. It is You, Lord, who will liberate the oppressed of Your people. You are the glory and the salvation, the One for which we have prayed. Now tonight, I will close my eyes and pass into the peace of God's Love." A tear from the man's eye fell into the open hand of God's child. At once, Jesus's little hand made a fist and He brought it to his open mouth. At this, the old man quickly handed the child back to me, then fell to his knees sobbing. Having known him all of his life, my dear father brought him up and helped him walk slowly, yet with new strength, into the Temple.

There were others who came near to see the child as we proceeded into the Temple of God. So much love was expressed when they saw Him. I could sense immediately the change in their hearts when they looked into His soft, sweet eyes. Each person, even unrealized, had a purpose that day in coming to the Temple. It was to meet the Son of God.

The priest of the Temple knew we were coming for the ceremony on that early morning. I pulled back the covering and when he saw little Jesus, at that moment, he stepped back and drew in a quick breath. He then opened his arms and prayed, pausing and thanking God for allowing Him to be his servant and fell to his knees before us, my dear father again helping another tribesman up from the ground.

Joseph had brought two doves in a wooden cage, covered with a cloth, for the sacrifice to be given. As he handed the birds to the Rabbi for the ceremony, a tear rushed from my eye. My mother reached out and squeezed my arm to stifle my cry. She knew my heart was in protest over this part of my tribe's rituals. I leaned closer to her and tightly closed my eyes. Little did I know that my own son would be the last of these sacrificial rites within our tribe.

After the ceremony, a few more of the people came up to see the baby Jesus, to give us blessings and tell us what a fine son we had. They both knew and did not know, that it was He that they were drawn to, the Son of God Himself, even as the Angels shielded His Light from their eyes.

The people then pressed into our hands offerings of money and refused our efforts to take them back, saying these words, "It blesses us to give, as we have received so much from our Father in Heaven. Please take what is given in gratitude to our God."

This of course, was God's way of providing for our long journey to Egypt.

Before we departed, my father counted the

money given to us as Joseph and I had asked, so that we might give a good offering to the Temple. An offering was also given to the priest for performing the sacred ceremony, which our family said was the most beautiful ceremony he had ever performed. I am certain that many families have thought the same of Holy ceremonies given for their children, and in this proud moment, we of course, were no different.

"No, I cannot take money for serving the Child of God," he shook his head and whispered to my husband. "Please take it, Rabbi," Joseph said, "as you do work tirelessly for our people and God would have it so."

It was a perfect morning for everyone and my heart was filled with gratitude and joy. I did not want this time to end, but I knew that it was time to make the journey of urgency to Egypt. It truly was the morning to leave my mother and father's home. God's child must be protected, not only by the Angels, but by borders of countries.

The Angels had protected us and veiled the eyes of those around us as we left, so that they would not follow or speak of our baby's presence, until long after we were gone.

As we set out on the road, for the first time, Jesus started to cry. He did not cry loudly, but enough so that I would rock, kiss, and sing to Him to console Him. My heart and mind was on His being at peace. "Shhh, my little one. God and His Angels are with you always." Soon I understood that it was not that He was uncomfortable, or in distress, but in the act of consolement, He knew that I was also consoling myself, because I missed my family tribe already. Even this young, so gentle and wise was He.

Egypt

Our journey to Egypt was not an easy one. Joseph and I were traveling into the unknown. It was a slow and arduous journey that would take many months. However, we knew that wherever we went and whomever we would meet, God would be in that place, giving us food and refuge when we were in need.

Knowing the history of our people, our coming to Egypt was a very timely one as well. The pharaoh had reluctantly released our people from slavery generations before. Even as the Jewish people were freed from suffering, the Egyptian people had suffered greatly. The enslaved Jews had hurriedly left in the darkness of that terrible time. Now Joseph and I, from the House of David, would bring into their fold the Light and the Liberator of the World.

* * *

There are those in the life, who ask to serve God, and when this prayer is spoken, when the asking is pure and sincere, the door opens wide without hesitation.

Their lives are burnished and fitted as a craftsman creates a sword. But the Server is a weapon for God's good work and his or her reward is a fullness of heart like none other. If you could see a fine sword made in this way, you could see that such a fitting, a life, is not made easily. However, many gifts, known and unknown, are bestowed upon the servant of God, as she or he becomes an instrument of His Love.

Such a person was Raheem, and his loving wife, Seeta. Raheem was tall and powerfully built. Seeta was half his size, with long, black hair and an engaging smile. They were humble, hardworking people, traders from Egypt, who a few months into our journey, began to walk with us, befriending us and showing us the way. We had been given directions before we left, but our new friends, having followed the trade trail many times before, knew the best way and became our guides, asking nothing in return. I knew the Angels were with us, protecting us and lighting our path, but as you know, human companionship comforts and teaches the heart.

Our new friends, of course, were God's gift, as friends often are. Raheem's constant conversation was refreshingly uplifting. The world was joyful to him. He never spoke unkindly about anyone, but he made all life around us seem less heavy, less serious. Raheem taught us to laugh.

"Well perhaps, laughter is God's recreation of the heart," he explained with a broad smile and great hand gestures. "And recreation is a taking off the burdens and creating anew!" With this, he laughed so loud, our donkey let forth a long, "Hoonk!" which made us laugh all over again.

Joseph asked Raheem, "Friend, what is your religion?"

He answered, "I am Egyptian, and we worship the Sun, the Moon, and other gods and goddesses alike, but more than this, we worship ourselves!" At this, he laughed even louder. Lovely Seeta shook her head and laughed, too.

It wasn't long before Raheem and his wife knew that we were carrying the Christ child and who we truly were. The Angels had told him in a dream the first night we met as we laid our heads upon the ground to sleep. On the next morning, he spoke to my husband. "I have had a dream. It was made known to me!" "Yes, my friend," Joseph interrupted, "I know. God has lifted the veil for you to see."

"Oh, I have been entrusted with the greatest of secrets!" Raheem exclaimed with as much of a whisper as he could possibly muster with his booming voice. And as tears of joy ran down from his eyes, he looked at my son and spoke these words. "All, all that I have is Yours, my Lord, and if I would see You in the flesh no more past this day, I will give all to others in Your name. No, not that I may gain earthly wealth, but only for the joyful upliftment of my heart, which I will also give to others!" "This!" he continued with a smile, "This is by the Grace of your God, and this is the life I shall henceforth lead!" At that moment, my son kicked off His covering and made a joyous, happy sound.

Then Raheem's wife came forth holding a small bottle of precious oil, and with my smiling permission, she rubbed and kissed His little hands and feet, the first of many others to perform this sacred deed. Thus began our long and happy friendship, my first with non-Jewish friends.

When we arrived in Egypt, I was amazed. The people were different, their buildings were different, and the way they dressed was different as well. Even the aromas of their cooking and the ways of their speaking were sounds and smells I had never known before. I was glad that Raheem had been our guide and had prepared us with his stories of the history and ways of his people.

Of course, the Angels never left us and our new friends brought us to their house. "This is your home now!" they exclaimed. "Please grace us with the acceptance of this gift to your son and his blessed family. It is now a Holy place by the presence of your feet upon the threshold. You will always find protection here."

Before entering the house one step further, we knelt down in prayer, thanking God for the blessing of this safe haven and for the gift of our new friends, who had brought us to their home. As we stood upon the warm tiles outside, we also gave pause, of course, to carefully wash our feet before entering.

It was a respectful and customary practice for foot travelers to wash their feet before entering a house. Water and sweet oils were ready for us, which felt so refreshing. Seeta, of course, did the task for Jesus, even though, not yet walking or crawling, He had no need of it. "Well, He needs to get used to this custom," she said as her excuse. She rubbed His little feet with her own special oils and kissed them once more. In return, Jesus gifted her with a delightful baby smile and a joyful squeal. With that, Seeta rose up and danced into the house. Her weariness from the trip was completely gone.

Dear Raheem had already sent a message to their servant to ready the house for us and to have a good meal prepared according to our religious standards. An astute trader, he even brought a few Holy Scriptures and had begun to set up a small corner as a prayer room for us. "There is a Rabbi in the nearby village," he explained. "I sent word that we would have guests from Jerusalem."

Holding Jesus, I looked into Raheem's smiling eyes and whispered a "Thank you. May God be with you always." Lightly touching our baby's cheek, he responded for the first time in a quiet, serious tone. "His religion is my religion now. Seeta and I are at His bidding." Jesus then closed His eyes and an indescribable peace filled the room.

After our quiet dinner, perfectly prepared by their servant, we were led to our room. We had the best sleep we had known in a very long time. Again, I heard the Angels sweetly singing "Rest now, dear Mary. Sleep, sleep, sleep for the protection of God is with you and beautiful morning comes soon." My peaceful child also slept all through the night.

For three days and nights Joseph, Jesus and I rested. When first we arrived in the evening, it was only one day away from the Sabbath, the seventh day for which God intended for our rest. The Sabbath, the practice of our people, was holy because God took His rest on the seventh day, after He had created the beautiful world. This we explained to Seeta and Raheem.

"What a wonderful Law of your religion!" Raheem said laughing. "It is a good one indeed!" And so, we rested the day after our arrival, then the Sabbath and the day after as well. Seeta too rested and even allowed her servant to work as little as possible and take some rest herself on these three days.

These restful times are good for the body and the soul. There are those who seem to fight against it, thinking that if they do more, they will have more money and more time for other things. They feel that the Law of Resting is a frivolous act and that perhaps they can get through life without it, or take as little of sleep and rest as possible. Health of the body and the mind are then at risk. What a loss when rest is ignored! The Law, which God Himself made Holy upon the creation of the World, as He rested upon the seventh day, is profound in its perfection.

Deep rest gives the body, mind and spirit time to pause. The body takes its healing in stillness and the letting go of the tensions held too long. The mind is allowed then to relax and find peace. The spirit also has, in this time, to emerge in its perfect form and be recognized.

So take the time, make the time to relax and see it not as an effort, a chore, but a blessing. See it as a time to allow the body, mind and spirit to work without working, toward healing and awakening to God's immeasurable Love and Wisdom within.

* * *

A change of life, staying for a while in a new place, a new country, I began to understand, is good for the heart and the soul. This is what beautiful Egypt was for us. God had brought Jesus, Joseph and myself into this land, not only for protection, but for many reasons and discoveries.

Truly, I had never been away from my tribe, my family. Even in the hills, as you know, I was always with my mother. I only knew my Jewish people. But on the route and staying in Egypt allowed Joseph and me to see and to accept that there was a different part of the world we had never known.

In our childhood, we had heard from teachers and storytellers, of other countries and the different people who lived there. Pictures were drawn in the sand, as the storytellers spoke of strange animals and huge structures shaped like triangles.

I, Mary, did not know or desire to see them as others did. I only knew in my heart, that my fervent desire was to see God and walk ever in His Light. Although I listened intently to the descriptions of other places, the outside world rarely passed my thoughts.

Now here we were, guided to seek refuge in this country, taken in by loving people who were strangers to us, but not to God. They were as humble Angels who walked the Earth. Raheem and Seeta were God-chosen. Therein we accepted and trusted our guided sojourn without question.

* * *

Early each morning, Jesus would awaken first. Even after He was bathed, fed and held in prayer, He would cry and cry until Joseph and I took Him out into the city to look upon the people. Peaceful at my parents' home while we were in hiding, in the mornings of Egypt, He was not!

We walked among the people in the morning hours and as young as He was, His eyes were wide open, looking, listening, taking all of it in. I am certain that Jesus looked more intently at the poor, the children, and the downtrodden.

The marketplace, the city was filled with people, more than I had ever seen in one place! Some here in this land, were far from their homes as we were. It both surprised and lifted my heart that no one seemed to mind or take note that there were those of different colors in skin and in clothing. Strangers would stop us to look at our baby and talk to us of their lives and oftentimes of their troubles, as God gave us the miracle of almost instantly of learning their language as they spoke.

Often, they would ask us who we were, where we came from, and why were we there. My dear husband, Joseph, would answer that we were travelers on a journey, deemed by God's Holy Grace. Some seemed to just accept this answer and some wished to linger, so to have a conversation to tell of their beliefs, as well as, to learn of ours.

This gave Joseph and me an opportunity to tell them of the One God who had blessed us and our people in so many ways and how much our faith meant to us, and that faith in our lives meant more to us than even the clothes we wore every day. Since Jesus would cry if we sent them away too soon, we also listened patiently about their gods and their beliefs. We wanted, needed, to understand one another, for in this way our hearts could grow.

Many would look into the smiling eyes of God's Son and begin to ask, "Please, could you tell me more about this Holy One that can be felt, but not seen?" And questions such as these which we would answer, as they stood before the child transfixed and transformed.

This is not to say that we were intent on converting people to our religion, our faith in God. Know in truth, that personal faith is just that, very personal and very delicate to the soul. Live your faith and allow your deep Love of God to shine through constantly, so that others will see and wish to walk that path as well. There is no argument when the light is allowed to shine through without force or worry.

Forcing your religion upon another is just the same as forcing a child to eat a food she or he has decided not to like. The child will spit it out, perhaps when you aren't looking. Then they may be angry that you have forced the food upon them. However, if the child first sees you enjoying the food, seeing that it makes you naturally happy to eat it, this then, is a better way to convince them they might try and enjoy it also.

So we shared our stories in the marketplace, while Jesus seemed to listen and learn. And yes, dear reader, He also gave healings. Not by word or sound, but only by the Divine Love that shined forth from His heart as the sad and the sick drew closer to see the Holy child.

At first, we were concerned and asked, "Please look, but do not come too close to the child. He is too young." But then Jesus would cry loudly, so that we quickly learned to allow them to touch his feet and tell him "Hello." It was a beautiful experience for me to see their faces melt into smiles of love as they looked into His eyes. There were some who seemed to feel just a little better, but most looked stronger and straighter and much brighter as they walked away.

I understood then, that some people may need healing, the healing of God's Love, but they are not yet ready for the cure. This is a process of healing as well. So at times, there is a period of soul learning that only a long illness can provide. However long or short that may be, depends upon the individual or even that individual's family or community.

The person who is ill, and know this – anger and selfishness can also be called an illness and can also be a reflection of his or her community. Therefore, to have a healthy, loving and happy community, we must be in service and love helping those in need, as Jesus did even as a baby in my arms.

We are all born in the time, which God has

provided for us to incarnate into this world. But truly at that time, as it is provided, we make a choice. We use the Law of Free Will to choose how we shall spend our time. We choose how we respond to the lessons before us. Growth of Spirit has three aspects: fast, slow and stagnant. If you knew how much joy there is being close to the Great Love of God, if you could comprehend its sweetness, your choice would be an easy one, my dear reader. This is my wish for you.

After the morning hours, when the sun was too high to cast a shadow, Jesus would fall fast asleep in my arms and only then we could take Him back to the house, which Raheem and his wife had so generously provided for us. We would tell Seeta and Raheem of the people we met and their stories.

In one of our encounters, a very wealthy man came to inquire about our presence in the city. We had noticed him several times before as he walked through the marketplace. The man was dressed in pure white, with perfect gold banding, which even in the dusty roads with people and animals moving about, never seemed to get dirty. His servant, with skin as dark as night, was always a few steps before him, bending and sweeping nearly every step of the wealthy man's path and wiping his swollen, sandaled feet with a long gray cloth, this the servant's only clothing which he wore around his waist.

Jesus was tiring as the hot sun was rising higher. We were about to leave when the man spoke, "Who are you? Why do you speak to so many people in this place and what do you offer?" "Kind sir, we offer nothing, yet strangers such as yourself, ask only for conversation and to look at the child," Joseph said, putting himself in front of me as I covered Jesus's head with a cloth to protect Him from the sun. "Well then! I shall look upon the child myself!" said the wealthy man. At that moment, Jesus began to cry loudly and knowing the meaning of this cry, I stepped forward, gently taking the covering away from His face.

The man's tired servant quickly moved aside so that his master could come closer. Jesus immediately quieted then and as the man's eyes saw Jesus, he drew in a strong breath and his hands quickly covered his face. Then looking deeply into the eyes of the Son of God he said, "Lady, I have never felt love before and with one look, this child has opened my heart. Please, speak to me of this power that your baby holds!" "It is a power that you also hold as the Loving God is as close to you as your now open heart," I told him. Therefore, he opened his purse, filled with gold coins, and offered it to us. "Here, please take all of this, and I shall bring you more!" Then Joseph, touching his shoulder said, "No friend, we are not in need of money, for God provides all that we need. With our faith, we are ever guided by Him."

The wealthy man then smiled and turned to his servant, giving him the entire money purse, "Take this and be free! I shall enslave you no more, for freeing you, frees my heart as well." And with that, the newly released slave stood upright and ran with happy shouts through the astonished crowd.

From our outings into the market square, we brought in the news of the morning, as well as needed spices and foods for the evening meals. Our descriptions of the beautiful city and its marketplace, where they both had lived all of their lives but were amazing to us, seemed to please them greatly. When we explained to Raheem how Jesus seemed to intentionally draw the people to Him for their healing, he then laughed out loud and said, "Only He would seek to work as a baby!" Jesus laughed too at the sound of Raheem's laugh, which made sweet Seeta dance and sing aloud as their young, black dog jumped for joy. How blessed we were to be guests in such a happy home.

* * *

Often times near the evening, before our hour of prayers, I would take just a bit of precious time to visit the animals while holding Jesus closely in my arms. The goats and donkeys were in a large pen next to our temporary home. Raheem and Seeta's dogs would always follow us outside to play and find relief.

Even if the animals were just being fed, when

they saw us coming, they would rush past their feeding bins to greet us. Jesus would laugh out loud at the sight of them pushing ahead to be near Him. He would put his hands to them, which the animals, crowding together, would lick and then push the top of their heads towards Him for a petting. "Oh, bless them!" I said one night. "Bless!" said the Son of God as His first word.

The feeling of Unconditional Love from these furry beings was near to God in my heart. I loved even the strong scent of them and the soft touch of their warm fur in my hands. I would softly hum songs of God's Love to them and thank them for their service, the milk, the carrying of our burdens and the feeling of quiet humbleness which they brought to our family.

"I will never eat you my brothers and sisters," I would say to the goats as my son and I rubbed their fur in mutual delight. "Only in gratitude will I drink of your milk." Then the goats and donkeys would press even closer, so that I might rub their backs as well, and tell them how wonderful they were. It is truth that every being thrives in the joy of positive and loving attention.

From the start, I convinced Joseph and Raheem that these goats would never be given for slaughter as food or sacrifice. I asked that even after their milk was dried, that they would be cared for with love to the end of their days. This was a promise from Raheem to me.

Of course, there were cats about as well. They served the household by keeping mice and rats away, and as Seeta said in sincerity, "Just by their royal presence we are honored!" Cats were highly revered by the Egyptians; and I will say, the Egyptian cat's purrs seemed quite extraordinary, soothing and melodic, as they sat warmly in our laps.

The three cats and the two dogs of the house, were drawn to Jesus of course, and were almost always at his side. It was difficult to know who was protecting whom, for if I pushed one of them out of the way, the crying of God's child would start once again.

Jesus' cries were not of the demanding sort as you might hear from a spoiled child. They were cries from a Divine Soul who already knew what was needed by those around Him. And I will let you know that from that time forward, the creatures of this household carried the gift of healing themselves and have passed it on to their offspring even to this day.

* * *

Jesus had reached the age of two, when I began to feel a deep longing to see my home in Jerusalem again. It was not just a passing emotional thought of missing my family as I had felt before, this was a strong pull which caused me to go outside in the night for seven nights in a row to look up at the stars in the East. I would pray and send love to my mother and father, asking that they be well and that they feel the love from my heart to theirs. I knew it was God's will when we would be returning, but I felt an anxiousness within my heart and prayed that it might be soon.

On the seventh night, an even stronger feeling woke me up again and I walked outside when everyone else was fast asleep. I looked to the Eastern stars and began to pray once more. Then before me an Angel appeared in a soft, blue radiant form. I felt upon me, a comforting Love and a gentle peace, letting me know that all was well in the home of my parents. I then fell on my knees and pressed my cheek to the ground thanking God for our friends, Raheem and Seeta and for the kindness of Egypt. I gave thanks for this place which had brought us such love, wisdom and safekeeping. I asked that Egypt and her people feel the outpouring Love from my heart and from the heart of my Holy son always.

Then the Angel spoke and said, "Rise Mary, it is time to bring your family home," and I was overjoyed. I gave praise to God, to the Angels and for the guidance and the message as well, of finally coming home.

I went inside and unable to sleep, I waited until

the first light of the sun brought the new day in before I woke my Joseph. "Yes Mary," he said. "In my dreams last night, the Angel told me the same. I feel your happiness," he said, smiling as he squeezed my hand. "We will leave for Nazareth the day after tomorrow."

Raheem and Seeta were to come home that day after a week of traveling and trading. As always, they sent their servant one day ahead to prepare for their homecoming. We always looked forward to seeing our friends after a trading journey. We loved listening to their stories and news about the world outside.

However, this time something seemed different about the way Raheem's servant was preparing the house. The tiny woman, whose language we could not speak (in the marketplace, in the city, those who touched Jesus, it was given us to understand) cleaned everything so that it shined even more. She was also attentive in preparing Seeta's favorite dishes to eat. There were almonds with goat's milk and honey, sesame cakes and figs stuffed with sweet curd.

Jesus, who stayed beside her as she was cooking, was given tastes of everything when she thought I could not see. Finally, I shrugged and smiled when she knew I had caught onto her secret gestures. She laughed to herself and gave Jesus a small cake, which of course, He broke in half and put the largest portion into her mouth as she picked him up to give him a hug.

"Jesus, Jesus, Jesus!" "Child, child, child!" she said lifting her voice, which dissolved into her own happy singsong language. Usually quietly cooking and cleaning the house, I had never heard her sing or say more than a few words before; and I found that she had a sweet uplifting voice that was delightful to the ear.

As she sang in her manner of words, in her uplifting tone, I began to sing in harmony, free and joyful praises to God as Joseph played his flute. We danced about the house lifting and passing Jesus back and forth, laughing, singing and twirling around. We felt that the Bright Angels were dancing with us on that happy day. This is one of my favorite memories of that time and I am happy to share it with you.

It was in the early part of the evening, as we were finishing our prayers and reciting the scriptures, when Raheem and Seeta returned from their week's journey. Their happy mood seemed to match ours, as we sat down to share the late meal, carefully prepared by their singing servant.

That night, the blessing of the food was said by Raheem, "Oh Heavenly Father, thank you for the food which You have set before us upon this table. Thank you for all of our blessings, known and unknown, today and in the days to come." He finished the prayer while gazing into my son's brown eyes. "In service, Lord all of ours is yours." Little Jesus then excitedly spoke the words, "Blessing, Raheem!" At that, Raheem and Jesus broke into laughter again as they had done at the table many times before.

Joseph asked Raheem, "Is it a celebration for your wife's birth anniversary, my friend?" "Tonight we are eating and truly enjoying all of her favorite recipes." Then Raheem leaned forward with Seeta smiling and holding his hand, "Well, my friends, this night we are celebrating that, after eight years of happy marriage, Seeta is with child at last!"

At this announcement, he playfully rubbed the top of Jesus's dark brown curls. "Your son Mary, the Son of God Himself, has brought a great healing into this home." He leaned back in his seat with his arms outstretched and boomed. "And we are gratefully blessed!" His wife of course, could not stop smiling and gave Jesus a tickling on his feet. I rose and hugged Seeta and kissed her cheeks. "How happy I am for you, my dear sister Seeta! All prayers will be answered for you." "God indeed has blessed us all."

After such an announcement, Joseph and I decided to wait to tell them the plans of our leaving. It was a joyful night and we felt that our news would not be as joyful. So, in respect, we kept our thoughts of going home to ourselves until the morning. It was of importance to allow our dear friends to have their moment of happy news without interference at all.

* * *

It was after our morning prayers with praise and songs of giving thanks to God for our blessings, that we told our dear friends of our visions.

Seeta started with quick tears, while Raheem let out a big sigh as he rubbed the side of his face. Then taking our hands, he said, "We knew these days with the Holy Child and His family would be short in time, yet we are grateful that is has been for this long. Our hearts have been turned to the Light of the One God, to the miracle of His Love and our lives have been changed forever more. For this we have been most blessed!"

I had already begun to pack and gone outside to sing to the animals the night before. Our own long eared donkey braded his approval and seemed ready to go. The sweet, black dog knew we would be leaving and whimpered at my side. "I am sorry to leave you dear Taz. You have been a good friend to me and my little one," I said as I scratched his ears. "But it is God's guidance that we follow always."

That day everyone was busy helping us to pack and to put our things in order. Of course, we had acquired more than we had brought into Egypt with us. A good friend, Raheem, would give us things that we needed, and did not need, as he and Seeta came back from their journeys of trading.

"Thank you, my brother," Joseph would say, "we have enough! The generosity of your food and home is enough for us." But Raheem's joyful and generous heart would insist and seek to bring us more. Therefore, we had extra clothing, oils and blankets, as well as, carved toys for Jesus to carry on our long journey home.

Raheem wanted to give me a necklace of gold with a beautiful Star of David and a tiny, bright emerald in the center, but I refused. "Thank you, my dear friend, but God is the jewel in my heart," I told him smiling and putting it back into his hand. "You know this to be true, but when I think of you and Seeta, I will remember the emerald and the star, for your friendship is true and never wavering."

Raheem then put the necklace around his wife's neck, which was already bejeweled from his many gifts, and laughed. "This one is from Mary, the mother of the Son of God!" It looked so beautiful on her and I said so. It seemed to carry the energy of her eyes, which were brimming with sparkling tears of joy and sadness.

Of course, Jesus knew we were leaving. There was nothing we could or would not keep from Him. He crawled and toddled around the house touching the walls and the stone floors saying, "Bless, bless house!" Taz the dog followed him from room to room, wall to wall, watching his every move. This did not go unnoticed by the servant, as everyone else was focusing on the upcoming journey. "Look! The child!" she said in her own beautifully lilting language.

Then, Jesus held the young dog's head in his little hands and said with the happy voice of a young child who could not contain his volume, "BLESS, BLESS!!" Now, I am sure you can guess, were it any other dog, or any other child, there would have been an instant parting of ways, with ears pulled back in pain, as the blessing was so piercing, so loud. But Taz jumped for joy, knocked the child over, and licked his face while Jesus laughed and laughed.

"Child, child, child!" said the servant pointing and laughing at such a happy sight. All of us laughed too. Watching intently Raheem said, "Well now, my favorite of all the animals." He knelt down to rub the dog's black fur belly, looked into Jesus's joyful, brown eyes and said, "This one," cocking his head toward Taz, "from my heart to yours, oh Holy One, a good dog!"

Jesus threw his arms around Raheem and said, "Raheem, Taz my dog!" We all laughed and had tears in our eyes too, as they embraced and Jesus's new pet ran happy, fast circles around them both. Then Joseph and I looked into each other's eyes, as parents have done for thousands of years before and since, with the smile that says, "How can you turn down such a gift of love, joy and protection for a child?" Of course, Jesus and Taz had decided long before anyone knew, that they were a pair.

* * *

Seeta woke us the next morning before light and hurriedly made breakfast as we said our prayers and packed the rest of our belongings. We needed to leave before the city woke up, looking for our presence in the marketplace, the presence of the Holy Child. We knew that many might follow us out of the city if they knew we would be leaving.

Of course, you can imagine how hard it was to say goodbye to our friends who had given and taught us so much, but God's calling, and the love of our dear family so far away, gave us the strength and the determination to do His bidding.

Raheem had told Joseph that the news from their travels was that although Herod had died a painful death, his son was now the appointed ruler of Judea. "The Angels, God's messengers, will tell us where to go as we journey to our land of Israel," Joseph said. "But it is dangerous my friends, do not yet go back to your home! Stay longer please." This was lovingly said in a very protective and fatherly tone. Besides a dear friend, Raheem had become just that, like a father to Joseph and me. He was wise, patient and concerned for our safety. But his eyes twinkled like a child's when he laughed and oh, we missed him already.

Through Raheem, we learned that God is indeed full of joy and that an expression of that joy to others, is a great service to humanity. Seek to find the joy in life, which God has given, and show it to others. A simple smile to those you meet along the way is a gift of upliftment and healing to the soul and to all the world.

Taz the dog, was ready to go, running back and forth, showing us where the road started. He had a job, a Holy mission and was happy for it to begin. However, we lingered a little while longer for extra prayers and hugs. "We will see you again, perhaps on one of our trading journeys." "We will send news of the baby's birth!" our friends exclaimed.

Raheem looked into the eyes of Jesus, as Seeta's eyes were wet once again. "I know I will hear great things of you, my Lord, for I have had dreams of you even before we met upon the road from Jerusalem!"

I looked up and thought I saw a faint ray of the morning sun's light on the horizon, a bidding of God to leave now. I drew in a quick breath. "Hurry Joseph, hurry my husband, it is now the time, it is time for us to go!" Joseph nodded and then without further question, we set out on our journey back to Israel, leaving our dear friends of Egypt behind with our new dog running straight ahead.

Along the way, a prayerful song was welling up in my heart and these words leapt from my throat. "From Thee and to Thee, Our God, the light is Thine! God the Good, the Holy One! Oh God the light is Thine!"

I knew that we were walking in the Loving Light of God and as we journeyed home, I felt little need to ride my donkey, as my feet truly did not feel the ground. I felt no weariness no matter how far we traveled and told my husband so. "My heart does lift me up," I exclaimed. "For I am to see my family once again."

"Mary, my love," Joseph whispered in my ear, "this is because the path is made Holy wherever you may walk." "And it is God's Love that has blessed me so, my dear husband." I squeezed his hand tightly then, as I felt so grateful for Joseph's steady, protective love.

Jesus, being so young, slept much of the way to Nazarcth, talking in His sleep in a language only known to him and His Father. The long journey home was uneventful, blessed and easy. Whenever we took our rest, we often left a few items along the way, giving blankets, food and coins that others might need along this well-traveled path, as others had given to us. As this was done, we always said a prayer that these offerings would go to the ones who needed them the most.

Giving from the heart, expecting nothing in return, brings God's Love ever closer to the soul's fulfillment of service. For it is in God's delight that we are born. Even at the start, our innocent hearts are filled with His Love. We are given a call to Love and to be in service to Him before we know these words - Service and Love.

It is deep within us that we hurt when others are hurt or in need. And this is the plan of God, that we might be part of the Force of Angels on this Earth. It is a calling, a stirring within to give, to awaken to the expansion of the heart. Know this to be truth, we can only feel the upliftment, the immersion of True Unconditional Love of the Highest Source when we seek to serve the Light. This service, this giving, can be as creative as the soul who gives.

It is the giver who seeks to serve in many ways, who is in partnership with the Creator Himself, and who in turn, receives a fulfillment that is more beautiful, more sacred, than any precious gem or gold. The joy you seek my dear reader, is the joy you seek to give.

Full Circle

As we walked toward Nazareth, finally nearing the village, I saw my mother running toward us, calling my name. With her long skirt disturbing and distributing the dust in the road, it was such a beautiful sight for my longing eyes. My smiling father strode quickly behind her; a long staff in his hand was pounding the ground as he walked. I was thrilled to be near my parents again!

So it was my mother who greeted us first as we entered Nazareth. These calling devices, these phones that you use, we did not need any of those. Heart to heart, our close family intuition was always clear. Our trust in God's guidance, our deep faith in His Love, left not a doubt within us, and as such, made our intuitive connection even stronger. I knew my mother would feel my love coming ever closer, even before we crossed into Israel, our home country.

"Oh Mary!" She exclaimed, "I arose this morning and was so happy, as I knew that this would be the day I would see you again! God is good! He has answered my prayers once more!" Our hearts danced as we tightly held hands and looked into each other's eyes, my mother and I.

My quiet father joyfully embraced us and then picked Jesus up from the ground in his great arms.

The Son of God threw his arms around my father and hugged him tight. Then Jesus leaned over and pointed to the dog and said, "Taz, good dog!"

"Oh yes!" my father said. "This is your friend, eh?" He knelt down and patted the dog's head. Taz immediately rolled over to have his belly rubbed as well and my father complied. There and then was a joyful understanding of the heart, between grandfather and grandson. Holding Jesus in his arms, my father Josiah handed my mother the walking staff he had carried and threw the child up into the air, catching his grandson and lifting him up once again with a hardy laugh.

It was wonderful to see such delight in my father's eyes. I had never before seen him display such outright joy and this filled my heart all the more. He had seemingly walked in pain as he came toward us. But now the pain was no longer, and he barely noticed the staff he had held a moment before. My mother smiled and nodded her head as if to say, "Of course!" as she hugged me close.

That evening Jesus, Joseph and I prayed and took our meal in our new dwelling, which my father had already begun to build for us. My parents' home was outside of the village, but ours, which was more modest, was located closer to the center of Nazareth. This I knew to be God's plan.

Find the center of a town, and you will find a special energy, pointed and focused, like the hub of a wheel. In your prayers, send perfect peace and balance to that center. For from that center is a great power radiating outward. Pray that that center be filled with the Holy light, so that the energy it radiates will be balanced and filled with healing Love.

Know that whether this center point is balanced or unbalanced will be reflected in the day-to-day vitality of that place. It may be a small village, the center of the world, or even the center of your own Self. Therefore, ask that God's eternal Love, His quiet, but incredible Glory, bring forth Healing, Love and Balancing in Its Radiance in and from that center.

Knowing me well, the first task my husband began after our Sabbath rest was to build a bigger and better pen and stall, as he knew more animals would come to live with us and be lovingly cared for. My parents had been working hard to prepare this small home for us. It was only two rooms, with an entrance door at the front and another entrance on the side of the main room, going into the sheltered courtyard. In the back was the animal pen where we kept our donkey and two milking goats, a gift from my father's herd.

The gift my mother, Anna, brought to me was the small loom from my childhood home. She had used it for many years and now it was handed down to me. As I sat down to touch it, to move my hands,

Jesus seemed to recognize it right away as I began to work the thread that my mother had already started. He turned his head when he heard the rhythmic clack, clack, clack. This was a sound he had heard in the womb, the rhythm of the loom and my humming along.

"Love mama!" Jesus said as he hugged me against my waist. I leaned forward and kissed his head, breathing in the sweet scent of my young child, the love from my heart washing over him. "Glory unto God!" I said, looking up and thanking her with a smile. "I am gratefully blessed by your gift my dear mother."

The lines in Anna's smiling eyes had become deeper and there were streaks of silver gray in her thick, black hair. She looked wiser and more beautiful to me than ever before. I told her this and how deep she was within my heart. Then, she bent down to kiss the top of my head, lingering there to breathe in and continuing the cycle of love.

* * *

Our neighbors were members of our tribe, friends and cousins, many I had known most of my life. God was the focus of our small village, and as such, all followed the Laws of Moses and sought to please Him through prayer rituals and service, as well as raising our children according to the tradition of our faith. Nazareth was quiet, not outstanding in its beauty or resources of trade. As it was hardly noticeable and very few Roman soldiers came through, it was the perfect place to raise the Son of God.

Through the guidance of God's great Love, Joseph, my parents and I raised Jesus in the ways of our devout Jewish teachings. We knew of our responsibility and that God had chosen us as a family for such a task. In His blessing, the Lord on High seemed to make it easy for us to raise His child. Our lives were quiet, and as we went about working at our daily chores, praying and giving gratitude, we lived modestly. We were far from being wealthy, but we had all that we needed. Things that we did not need did not fill our humble home. Our lives were simple and we were happy and blessed in the Grace of God.

Joseph, who took his trade as a builder, had work that was steady. His skills were always praised and in demand. Making his own tools, strong and sturdy buildings were crafted by his hands. As Jesus grew, he worked side by side with Joseph and would always ask for the hardest task, even when he was still young and not yet able to pull the ring of a door.

I watched my son closely and I understood what He was striving for: to make himself as strong as he could, to help as much as possible, and to surmount any hardship put in front of Him. No, not for the sake of pride or ego; I knew he was in preparation, getting ready body, mind and spirit for the future, for the hardest task of all, the taking on of His purpose, for bringing the Light of God, for the healing of this world.

Our tribe, our people, through many generations seemed to be constantly fighting, always needing to defend themselves against occupation and oppression. Sadly, the stress which was felt from these outside forces brought division, fear and bickering, even between our own people. Under this pressure, a hard life was made even harder to bear. Therefore, we looked for peace, we prayed for a Messiah as God had promised in the stories, the writings, the scriptures left by our ancestors.

I knew this to be my son, that it was He who would change the world from brutality to love. But of course, dear reader, there were those among us who did not want this peace, tolerance and love – even neighbor to neighbor. And sadly, it is so now in your day. For peace brings ease and there is then no need for fighting, no need for war.

Those within our own temples saw that a Messiah of peace might depose them. Priests and leaders of the people feared a future without fighting, without people, full of fear, who were easily led and looked to them as powerful. In their hunger for power, they were blind to the Will of God, unable to see that the adorations they sought would have been even greater through good will and generosity for their followers.

Leadership based on fear and untruth is like a house built without a foundation beneath it. In time, the blind ones will crumble into dust, swept away by the winds. The leaders of fear will be left powerless with nothing to cling to having turned away too long from the Light of God.

* * *

As urged by Joseph and my father, they and the Rabbi of our village would come together, after prayers and the evening meal, to sit with Jesus and talk about the history and the laws of our people, in order to teach him our history, as well as, the scriptures and the rituals and of their purpose. These teachings began when Jesus was about six years of age and continued on for many years.

Now a child in his or her development has an anxiousness within. This is a gift from God, that they might have an urgency to ask, to experience, and therefore, to learn about the world in which they live. For Jesus in His youth, this was so and also not so. He would ask a question and then almost immediately begin to answer it in a way that clear and complex at the same time. In this way, the teachings that were presented brought new learnings of old lessons. So as the men were discussing the scriptures, Jesus so young, would soon become the teacher. He had a nickname, as you might say, within our village. He was lovingly called, Little Rabbi.

Of course, as you can imagine, these discussions went on at great length. Surprises, arguments and agreements of the interpretations were glorious to my hungry ears. These evening conversations were intense, loud, reverent, joyous, quiet whisperings of humble prayers and tearful as well. However, when the hour was late and the time for bed drew nigh, it was the animals of our home who let us know. First the donkeys started to bray and Taz, ever the faithful dog, would begin to circle the men. Then he would pull gently at first, then with meaning, on Jesus' cloak to come inside. It was time for the Holy child and His protector to curl up and go to sleep. The Rabbi would bow and quietly gather up his scrolls. Walking home, almost transfixed, he held those precious scriptures close to his heart.

* * *

Clear nights before the Sabbath, when all preparation work was done, were often the most special times for me. My mother, Anna, Jesus and I would set aside an hour of being outside together just looking up. Sometimes Anna would send a message that she was too tired to come, but truly I knew what she meant. "These times alone with your young son are sacred and precious. They will not last for long," she said. "Boys especially grow quickly in their independence from their mothers and this is God's good plan," she wisely said. "And Jesus, the Son of God, of course, has the most urgent of callings to go out into the world."

On the night of His seventh birthday, it was clear, cold and very dark outside and I knew the stars would be brilliant. By happenstance, this night of his birthday was the quiet evening before the Sabbath.

My Joseph was already fast asleep. He was a hard, diligent worker and this day of rest was most blessed for him, which he always honored by going to bed immediately after our prayers and the evening meal. We slept in the only private room in our very modest dwelling and Jesus slept in the main room in the center part of the house.

All of us had worked hard that day, but I could not sleep or even close my eyes to rest. I could feel God's love burning within my heart. The joy of It kept me awake, so I arose to see the stars on the anniversary of that very special night.

Jesus heard me as I walked into the main room toward the door to the outside. He sat up and softly said, "Oh, yes Mother, you want to see it too!" So, I took his hand and we went outside to look up.

Jesus brought the blanket from his bed and we lay on the ground to get a better view of the stars. On the night of his birth, they looked exactly the same, except for the bright, bright star which had called the shepherds forth, as well as the very wise men who had blessed and protected us.

"Here," I said, "this is the way the stars were positioned when you were born." As I was explaining to Jesus, I moved my finger up to the sky, pointing from one beautiful star to another. I continued, "These stars, they tell the story of you, the greatest blessing from God to mankind."

"Yes," He said in a whisper and then a pause. "Yes, I know." He squeezed my hand and laid his head against me. "I remember."

We watched the stars for a long, long time together, undisturbed, even by the faithful, black dog, usually close to Jesus's side, who wisely took his sleep in our house that night. Good Taz seemed to know how precious this quiet time alone would be for us.

"The stillness, the darkness is so profound this night," I said with a sigh and a smile. I felt such a blessing of peace and comfort then, next to the warmth of my Son. Only moments later, Jesus sat upright. "Out of the darkness, shines the light!" laughed Jesus, as He held out his hand, gesturing to the first rays of the sun rising in the horizon. "Time goes by so swiftly, my Mother." It was the most glorious sunrise I had ever seen. And of course, He was right.

* * *

Indeed, it seemed that time on this earth did go by too fast for us. I watched as my son grew taller each year. Taller than any of the men within our tribe. Or maybe it was the way He carried Himself, his skin, his sweet, knowing eyes, and even his dark curly hair always beaming a soft radiant light. But this is from a mother's eyes as I am telling you of His countenance.

As the years slipped by, He also grew farther away from our family and closer into God's light toward the work which He was sent to do. Watching Jesus grow, my heart was both heavy and glad at once. It is difficult for any mother to see her child begin to take the first steps away from her heart. Even though I knew it was God's will, my own was increased by the knowledge of His purpose which, I knew, would require more strength than anyone before him or after would ever bear.

Jesus's studies with our Rabbi, Joseph and my father became ever more frequent, as well as His time in the Temple. Always attentive and kind, Jesus would let us know that He would be gone a day or more, but soon, we were assured, He would return home. "I feel a calling from other teachers now," He would say, and we understood.

These outings began about the age of ten, but I could see it coming. At nine years old, he would sometimes walk our visiting Rabbi back to the Temple at night as they continued to talk about

God's Love and Laws with excitement and reverence, sometimes returning only in the morning.

At the beginning of Jesus's journeys away from us, I was asked by some of the women in our village, as I would go to the well to draw water, "Your son, the Little Rabbi, has walked far from your house and has been gone now for days, are you not worried? He is so young!"

"He is doing what is rightful for Him to do," I would say. "God's Angels will surely watch over Him, and Joseph also has given Him his blessing." Then I would ask, "Will you come over for morning prayers tomorrow? Your mother and children are welcome, too." And speaking thus, at once they were at peace.

Now, those in the village could not yet see who Jesus was, as God had not revealed Him to their eyes. However, it was clear to me, that in the times He would be gone, even unrealized, all were looking for Him to return. They did not think about the Presence, the Light, the extraordinary peace that He carried until it was not there.

* * *

On early mornings when Jesus was away and Joseph began his day of work, building repairing homes and structures in our community, my mother and other devoted women of our tribe would come by to sit in prayer together. "How is your son, Jesus?" was the question as they arrived. "When will He return?"

My mother and I would exchange knowing glances then. We knew that where He was, and when He would return, was according to God's Plan and was not dictated by the time of our world. Even so, we missed Him as they did. "By God's Grace, he will return very soon and in good health," I would answer with a smile, and then lead them in quickly to read the Holy Scriptures and say our prayers inside.

In the middle of our circle, we lit the lamp carefully, giving gratitude to God for all of our blessings, speaking them aloud, but in a quiet nature to give them power. Then as we continued, some prayers were said in silence, while some were spoken aloud, according to the one who carried them.

Within the circle of women, our respect and understanding for one another was unmeasured. This we knew: we are all the same. All were seeking to open to the Light of God within our time, as you, dear reader, do so in yours. Those who do not believe, secretly wish for it to be true. Those who believe, wish for the Light as well. They seek the Illumination of God's Love. So then, we are all the same.

It is the seekers who have the advantage, of course. They seek the tools that will help them to open the door, to let in the Holy Light. Perhaps just a small crack in the beginning, but in that moment, that first small, fleeting awareness of "Oh there! It is the Light!" the seeker awakens, as the heart leaps in fullness and the path therein cannot be denied.

Now it is true that only young boys were formally trained to read and write. However, it was the women who also brought their daughters into the Holy circles to learn to read the writings of our tribal ancestors, the stories of God which were lived and told of so long ago.

Joseph and Jesus knew of these meeting times of the women in our home. We never kept secrets from each other. How could we? Respectfully however, they kept away from our home during this hour, in understanding and approval of our women's sacred gathering.

In our circle, some of the women copied the scriptures. Knowing their importance, we placed them in dry urns to preserve them from the weather and from those who would destroy them if they were found in our possession. Some of those who were feared were husbands and relatives of the women who left with baskets of cloth and materials for sewing and weaving, their precious writings carefully hidden inside.

Now, in these times, the only freedom many women of our community had then were within these circles. Some women of our tribe were not allowed to come at all and we prayed especially for these.

After our prayers, we read, talked softly, and studied together, while a few sat in silence just to listen. On some mornings, no talking was needed for we knew that everything would be spoken in prayers. There was no judgment; only a few rules were needed for structure and protection. We were to come on time, in gratitude, in strict secrecy, in community, knowing the Grace of God had brought us together; that we were His children and that the giving of our hearts in service to others was the debt we gladly paid in the receiving of His blessings.

Often, the quiet discussions which followed were how best to serve God within our tribe and how to open our hearts to His guidance and Love. God's wisdom is often expounded within the conversations of friends who are close to us. As Joseph and I learned in Egypt, people who are not like us, who are not of our own tribe, can be our greatest teachers. Therefore, I was glad to share stories of the different sights, smells, animals and people of Egypt; as well as, of Raheem and Seeta, for speaking of them brought the joy of their friendship back to my heart.

Our time was limited, urged on by the flame. We kept time by the lamp, filling it with a measured amount of oil. Thus, when the flame began to lower, it was time to close, filling our urns and baskets and leaving the circle together and quickly.

Of course, our daily lives were not easy. We made our own clothing from gathering wool, to spinning, to loom. All water was brought from the well for cleaning, drinking and preparing food. So our service was in helping our friends, neighbors and families and one another in that time. Our writing, copying and preserving the scriptures was also a service to God, whom we knew in our hearts had asked for this endeavor to be done with love and diligence, even as it was done one task, one short hour at a time.

The devout, even in their weariness of daily living, did what they could to help others, as they felt guided to do. In a time so restricted by the constraints of day-to-day living, there was little time to go beyond our lives to learn of, or to help anyone outside our world, as you are so blessedly able. Here also was the occupation and the rule of the Romans. Our Jewish people had endured wars and oppression for many generations.

This is why Jesus, as He began God's work, was known as the Savior, in that He came to awaken humanity from the slumber that only our moment-to-moment, day-to-day, lives mattered. He gave us compassion and strength and awakened us to the realization that we mattered also to God. That all of us are filled and could be fulfilled in God's Divine Love every moment, day and night. What an awakening. What a great healing from the Loving Spirit!

Beloved, there is no comprehension of the Love which God has for you. Jesus was the messenger, the ambassador of that Love, so I will add to the Scriptures this:

In the beginning God said,

"Let there be Light."

And there was Light.

And then God said, "Let there be Love."

And there was Love.

Let the Light of Love illuminate your birthright,

Let God's Love for you light your way.

* * *

I knew the time had come, when I saw that Jesus was ready to begin God's work, to at last reveal Himself, to walk among the people and teach. He had been preparing for this revelation every day of his young life, as I have told you.

As He grew past twelve, we did find him in the Temple astounding the elders, citing scriptures and interpreting their meanings faster and more deeply than the most learned priests, who were both amazed and disturbed by His brilliance. This He would do so from that time forward as you know.

In the years as Jesus grew, more and more of our tribe came to see Him for His wisdom, as well as, for His kind words. Even as a baby in Egypt, the healing of the hearts came first and for many, these were miracles indeed. He began to bring the people's hearts to the awareness, the meaning of the scriptures, and to the Love of God, which was closer to them than they knew.

It was time to feed the souls, hungry for the Healing Light. "You must have faith, for God the Father loves you. Set your sights only on Him and turn away from the burdens which distract you," He would say, and the words offered from His voice were like healing honey on a wound. It was God's voice speaking to them and their eyes and hearts began to wondrously open. I saw that it took only a few words such as these to bring the understanding and awakening of the soul, so that healing and right action could easily come into their lives. The pain was gone and their walk was straight again, both in body and in Spirit.

Now the faith which He spoke of had not the meaning of just an idea, a thought that might possibly be true. It is this: a knowing, a feeling within of the Living Presence of God. Some are born with this knowing and for some, it is a path, a seeking, a goal to attain which may take many years or only just one day. So, here, dear reader, I offer to you a meditation which can bring that feeling of faith and knowing into your heart and your soul, which Jesus spoke about.

Dear one, as Jesus said, when you pray, go within a private place and close the door. Then your Father who sees what you do in secret will reward you. What is the reward? Enlightenment. A closeness to God that will never leave you.

Therefore, find a quiet place and a time to pray. Sit, relax, close your eyes, and twice from your heart, slowly say this prayer: "It is my fervent desire to meet you in this time, dear God, not for my own sake only, but also for Thine."

Take some time to feel the peace, the silence surrounding you. Let thoughts and sounds come and go as they will and know that there is no need to attach yourself to any of them now. Begin to feel the Grace of God's perfect Love ever so gently surrounding you, comforting you, giving you Healing, giving you Peace. Allow this sweet energy of Grace to go wherever it needs to go, without concern, without your direction, filling your entire being on every level. Sit in this blessing of Grace for a few sacred moments or as long as you like.

Then easily bring your awareness to your heart. Pause and feel your heart becoming full with the Unconditional Love of the Divine One. Feeling this, begin to connect the Love in your Heart with the Heart of God. Heart to heart, filling your heart with the Light. Continue for as long as this feels comfortable and right for you.

Dear reader, this can be a very powerful opening, so just a little emotional upheaval could occur, but with daily practice, this will change to Heavenly Bliss.

Upon ending the session, place your hands upon your heart, feeling the calming, the healing and the gratitude to God for this gift of Love.

* * *

Now, as soon as Jesus became a young man, He told Joseph and myself, that He must now go deep into the desert, as His Father was calling Him forth. As you know, we were familiar with His going away for days, and even weeks at a time, but Jesus had never mentioned a journey such as this, and in His voice, I could feel the gravity of it. I knew this to be His time of initiation and of His final leaving of our family home.

My heart was opened to the reality of what was meant to be and I was both grateful and sad together. We had made a promise, Jesus and I both, from the day we were born, that we would go without hesitation, whenever we were called by God, to whatever task He would put before us. I slowly let forth a deep sigh, a breath of letting go, and I bowed my head in the awe and wonder of God's great works to come. And at that moment, I felt a faint movement, a quickening within my womb, the tiniest of flutters, a precious, precious gift of God's unmeasured Love.

I had told no one of my pregnancy, I wanted to wait a little longer, but Jesus knew it then. He put a gentle hand on my belly and just said, "Mother." There was such a smile between us: one son in utero and the other about to go out to the world. I was finally pregnant with Joseph's child.

And then He left. Joseph squeezed my hand as we watched Jesus go, walking steadily, with an assured gait, taking nothing with him but his cloak and his walking staff, given to him by his grandfather many years ago. Taz, his good dog, had passed on a full year before.

I turned to look at Joseph and saw a tear fall from that big man's eye. "Fear not," I told him, "for we know that God and His Angels are with Him. It is His time." "And my husband," I said, patting his great chest with my hand, "I am with child and I know it to be your son."

Suddenly he laughed and said, "Oh Mary, I am losing my ability to dream!" I did not know this to be so!" He took me into his arms and danced me joyfully about the room. "I shall work no more this day. It is a day to see to your needs and to doubly celebrate the Glory of God's good works!" And this we did.

Now to be sure, Joseph did not lose his ability to know God's messages through his dreams. Nor did he lose his sense of levity. All was revealed to him as it was planned in God's time. My dear, faithful Joseph knew this as God's truth.

Those who are devout and trust in God's Love become more and more aware of these messages, this guidance, as it comes in many ways. Through dreams, omens and the whisperings of Angels, as well as signs which you feel in your heart to be true. Never doubt that following the path of God will bring a lifetime of understanding, wisdom and joy as well. Therein, even when worry besets you, the knowing of God's Heart brings peace beyond words to those who seek His Truth.

The first child of Joseph and mine was indeed a son, James. Our daughter, Sarah, came soon after. In all our children were three - including Jesus, Son of the Most High. Each one was a blessing from God, sent to us for joy and comfort in our lives. While Jesus was a Living Glory to the world, our children, Joseph and mine, were sent to us alone.

* * *

As time passed, we heard of Jesus's works among the people and the miracles He performed. Occasionally, and of course, not often enough for my mother and me, our family would meet Him in secret, since He could not come close to our home, knowing the crowds would follow Him wherever

He went. Even though the Angels did protect us, His Light had become much too brilliant to be unnoticed. And yet the Angels did bring the veil of protection around us, so that the crowds did not beseech us, even as we walked among them to hear Him speak.

It was Jesus's own siblings who were among the children, that His disciples, not realizing they were of His family, tried to keep away, when He said, "Let the children come to me, do not hinder them, for the kingdom of heaven belongs to such as these." Oh, how they loved to hold His hands and be held close in His arms! My heart would swell almost to bursting at this happy sight.

* * *

One early morning as I was walking back to our home with the children, bringing the water of the day from the well, I saw my Mother running towards me. "Oh, dear Mary, your father sleeps and will not wake!" she exclaimed in labored breath. "Yes, I am coming, my mother!" I replied. My father had been ill for many days and I took the children to the home of a friend and then ran the length of the village back to my parent's home. No time was so important as to be with my mother and my father, as I knew this to be his time of passing.

As I entered the house, I could hear the birds sweetly singing and the soft humming of my mother's servant, as she knelt at the end of my father's bed and carefully washed his feet with fresh water and sweet oil. My mother, Anna, was standing at his head, softly running her worried hands through my father's hair, looking only at him.

Overcome with sorrow, I bent down and lay my cheek next to his, my arms around his frail body. I could feel his heart barely beating. My tears wet both my face and his. "Oh father, how I wish Jesus was here this day to heal you!"

In a whisper he spoke, "Dear child, He is here by my side, as you know. He is here not to help me to live, but to help me leave this old body in peace. I feel such peace now my Mary and I am ready." His breath and whisper paused in my ear for a moment. "Oh, Mary, such peace, such love! Do not grieve my daughter. This..." With a faint smile he pushed his head deeper into my mother's hands, and he was gone.

His soul was lifted up by the Angels who had been with him all of his life, as well as the Angels of Jesus. I looked up and there He was, God's Son, by the bedside of my father, His subtle but powerful presence lighting up the dim room, like the soft sunlight in the evening. He had appeared for His grandfather, a great, strong servant of God and the rock of our family, whom Jesus dearly loved.

It was my mother's servant who shook and wailed. I stood and held my mother, softly crying in my arms, both of us remembering the decades of love they had shared together, of all that he had built for our family.

The servant's loud wailing was a calling, an alarm to our village that my beloved father had died. Soon the house was filled with friends and relatives to comfort and care for our family, as well as to perform the rites and rituals of our custom. The first part of the ritual was not to speak until the preparing of the body was performed, so that only tears were heard. But we told no one of the presence of Jesus at my father's passing until now, as I am relating it to you.

I stayed with my mother in my childhood home for many weeks, never leaving her side until she was ready. Ready to pull back the heavy wool from the windows and doors, to allow a glimmer of the day's sun to shine in. "I know, being a devout man and a good husband, father and grandfather, he is now in God's grace and Love completely, but oh, how I miss the presence of that wise and quiet man," She would say. Then I would sit close to her again, holding and gently stroking her hand to soothe her heart.

It was a sad time and I knew that I could not leave my mother to live alone. Therefore, it was decided that our family would move into her house, the home of my childhood. There was more space in this dwelling and our family, of course, had grown larger with our growing children. So it became a happier place for my mother in her last days.

The move was indeed significant for me. Physically, as our family had grown larger, but also emotionally, as Anna and I had always been so very close. Not just as mother and daughter, she was also my confidante and my Spirit Guide, my Earth Angel and my true friend. Now she needed me even more, as well as the love of my children. We had come full circle, she and I, as often happens in the Holy Cycle of Life.

The small dwelling we had lived in was never left behind. Joseph and I kept it, so that it could be used as a sanctuary, a sacred site for the devout women in our tribe. It was known in the village only as a place where women would gather to weave, dye and repair clothing together. However, this was also kept as a secret sanctuary where we could gather in circle, as before, to pray and counsel together. We were also now just beginning to learn about the teachings of Jesus, whom His followers were calling the Teacher, the Messiah, the One who was sent to us by God.

Only a few in this circle knew that I was Jesus's mother. As I have told you, God placed a veil over their eyes. We were protected by the Angels and in that knowing, I never felt afraid.

A younger woman, also called Mary, came often and became a dear and helpful friend to me. Her love for my son, Jesus, was beyond teacher and devotee, as she became His confidante and His caretaker, His close friend and His beloved. For this I was happy, as I knew her to be pure of heart, sent by God for His comfort and gladness, especially in the difficulties He would have to face.

The opening of our previous home for women to gather together was God's blessing for us all. Beyond the prying eyes of the men who ruled over our lives, husbands, relatives, priests and soldiers, the women of our village were able to express themselves more freely and creatively through reading, writing, and even song. I will say that the Love and Light which shines from a newly awakened soul is the most beautiful sight of all, and my eyes and heart saw many of those who were gathered together in that time of the emergence of Christ.

These awakened ones within our circles, these women, were joyfully in awe of the works of Jesus as they saw Him amongst the people or heard about His teaching and healings from the young Mary, as she and her sisters would speak in the circle. In the morning gathering, they would whisper stories such as these, "Oh, He speaks of God, even to the women around Him and He asks them to leave their work and stay in the room as He teaches!" "He saved my friend from being stoned to death!" And, "By touching his cloak, my mother was healed of her affliction!"

It was a time of elevation, of wonder, and of new hope for us all. My heart was full of love and joy for God's Son and for the world. My son Jesus was the Truth and the Light, sent so generously by God to this world. "Come into my heart and see the miracles of Love, as I enfold you in my Grace." This was the message, the Light which God gave by sending Jesus, the Messiah and the Christ, to heal the wounds of the world.

I knew this to be so from the beginning, from the very night the Light of Pure Love came upon me on the shores of Galilee. And now the weight of the world had begun to fall upon His shoulders. Although I needed no one to tell me about the crowds that followed Him, the miracles of healing by touch and word, the love and the fear of His works, I listened patiently to the stories and saw that they were written. Joseph, within his dreams, knew this as well, and my own loving Angels had revealed to me, long before my beloved son left our home, His works among the people yet to come.

I was acutely aware of those, even of the high priests, our own people, who sought to do Him harm. I understood that many of those who feared Him had false hopes of power, which they feared to lose. Therefore, they sought to extinguish His brilliant Light, not realizing that His Light, which no shadow could ever darken, was truly eternal. Every moment of His life was in God's Plan. God was in Him and He was in God.

Oh, how magnified in power they would have been if only they had truly given their hearts to Him in Love! Sadly, for those who were blinded with selfishness and fear, this was not to be, and I have truly wept for them as well.

The Offering

Our winter had passed and the days were becoming warmer. It was early morning after the full moon when it began to rain. The clouds had come in suddenly, as if appearing out of nowhere. A bright morning had quickly become much darker. Joseph was then too old to work at his trade, so after our morning meal and prayers he went back to his bed to rest again. Our son, James, was preparing to feed the animals.

I was sitting in my prayer corner, praying and making an offering upon the altar. My offering was of a feather, which I had found on the path as I was carrying water from the well the afternoon before this day. It was the most beautiful and perfect white feather I had ever seen. Turning it over in the sunlight, it seemed the soft edges shone a golden color. So I picked it up and tucked it inside my cloak, next to my heart so that my hands would be free to carry the water vessels. I thought, at that moment, how glad I was that Joseph had agreed that we would never sacrifice any of our animals since the blessing of Jesus when He was a baby at the Temple.

Seeing any animal suffer needlessly was too much for me. The people in our village would often bring their sick and wounded creatures to my home.

I would simply clean and bind their wounds while singing softly to them, allowing them to feel the Love of God pouring from my heart to theirs. The Unconditional Love these defenseless animals give in return is a purposeful, healing gift directly from God's heart and I delighted in each and every creature that I could hold.

Lighting blazed throughout the sky at the very moment I laid the feather on the altar. The rain started to pour and thunder roared loudly, startling and waking every animal and child in Nazareth. I then bowed my head and began to cry, for I knew this was an omen.

As I hung my head in tears, an Angel did appear before me. "Yes Mary, your son has been taken. His time is nigh. But take heart and fear not, for He is the Son of God and this is His purpose of Love. Now go to Him dear Mary. He is looking for your presence as comfort."

As quickly as these words were spoken, my body and my heart were lifted by the Angelic Force. I stood upright in that room of many prayers and said to God, "I am ready."

I said to my daughter, who was already standing by the door, "Tell your father I have gone to be with Jesus as He needs me now." I knew my sleeping husband would understand. He had slept through the thunder and was probably dreaming of my journey now. Therefore, he knew I must go alone.

One of Jesus's closest disciples, John, met me on the path as I was leaning forward, hurriedly pulling my donkey behind me. "Oh Mary! Mother of the Son of the Highest. Jesus of Nazareth, He has been arrested!" "Yes, dear one," I said. "I am coming to him by God's word." And we quickly walked together.

Along the way, I said a prayer. "Dearest Lord God, my legs and feet are aching as I am now old, but by your word, I know it is Thy will that I am carried to Him." Only moments later, a Roman soldier came upon us on a great horse, loudly asking who we were and where we might be going. By this time, the news of Jesus's arrest had spread across the land and many people had begun to walk on the path to Judea.

The soldier blocked our way upon the path. His demeanor was near to brutal in his design to make us fear his authority. But the horse he rode upon then sharply turned his head as I began to speak of my name and of our purpose. The strong, black horse looked straight into my eyes and said unto my mind, "I know you! This man has been a cruel master. But, you are well loved and known among many of the animals here. I will take you to your Son, oh Mother of Kindness and Healing."

Tears burst in my eyes and I gasped as the steed

knelt down and rolled his body over, so that the astounded soldier fell to the ground and ran away. God had allowed him, finally, to hear the words of his horse's lament.

Our new friend shook his body, as if to let go of his past trials with the soldier and released a happy neigh. "My caring one, I am so grateful for your service. God, Himself will reward you," I said, as John and I gladly climbed upon this kind animal's back.

While I took the burden of small supplies, a blanket, water and a heavy cloak, from my sweet donkey's back, I bent down and urged him to go back to our home. I knew he would find his way unharmed, protected by the Angels of the Beasts. Thinking that it would be late into the night before we reached Jesus, we were now within just a few hours as we rode upon our fast and sturdy steed.

(Dear reader, here much as in the beginning of writing Mary's story, I was very hesitant to continue. I was afraid it would be too difficult for me emotionally, and I felt I couldn't go on. My heart was racing and I could not stop crying. In an effort to calm down, I took a break from writing and that night I picked a random book from my bookshelf to read, which I had not done in a long time. As I sat down and opened the book, a bookmark with the picture of the Apparition of Christ at the Chalice Well, fell into my lap. [The explanation of this amazing bookmark is in the epilogue of this book]).

Light, as I had never seen, shined from this photograph, this blessed likeness of Jesus. And even though the picture was taken during the day, the sky was in darkness right behind Him. Then He said, with such Love to my heart, which made me smile and cry again at the same time, "Write Elizabeth, for from the darkness, shines a Light so Bright that it uplifts the hearts of the World!" With my strength returning, I said, "Yes, my Lord, I know it is Your will."

The Crucifixion

The sun, an enormous circle of red, blazing through the clouds, was starting to sink into the horizon of Jerusalem as we arrived outside its city walls. The young Mary and her sisters ran toward us, asking no questions as to why were on the back of a Roman horse. "Oh Mother", she said, as she choked back the tears, which had smeared the dirt on her face, "He will be crucified! Come, come!"

As we reached the summit and looked upon terrible Golgotha where tortuous crucifixions often took place, the darkest night fell just as they lifted him up on the cross. The disciple, John, now sobbing, and the young, weeping Mary slowly led me in as I sat upon the horse. I could not walk. Covering my eyes, I could barely see and I was unseen. All eyes were upon Jesus, my son and God's.

Then the noise of the crowd, which I had just heard screaming and crying, fell into silence. It was late afternoon, but the black night raced in early, casting a heavy veil and covering the land in sorrow. No one could speak. Even as mouths would open, not one could utter a word. I heard only soft sobbing and fires being lit to burning for warmth and light in the early pitch-black darkness.

My kind horse let me down near to the cross

where I heard my son breathing heavily and bleeding from his wounds. The Angels gave me strength and sight as our eyes met. A fire, freshly lit near the cross, was reflected in His deep brown eyes. There was a flash, a moment of remembrance of comforting love, as we both looked up at the stars to remember His story, to reaffirm this time of purpose and for strength from the Heavens. "My Son and my Lord, we are magnified in your Holy Love!" I said as I fell onto my knees.

Bearing the pain upon the cross then, slowly and with care, Jesus spoke to each disciple in turn, and to each man on the crosses beside Him. Each disciple received a message of Love, personal as well as strengthening to each one. Some have recorded their message in scripture, which you may have read, and some held theirs secretly in their hearts. Therefore, I will not reveal all here that I heard in His counsel.

He spoke as a friend and a teacher until nearly the last breath left His body. Always the Rabbi, God's beloved Son hung His head down and spoke the song of David, a song of anguish, as well as praise, which of course, He knew by heart from His childhood.

"My God, my God, why have you forsaken me? Words of my groaning do nothing to save me. My God, I call by day but you do not answer, at night, yet I find not respite. Yet You, the Holy One, who make Your home in the praises of Israel, in You our ancestors put their trust. They trusted You and You have set them free. To You they called for help and were delivered. In You they trusted and were not put to shame. The whole world will remember and turn to God. All the families of nations will bow down before Him!"

Finishing these words, He asked for His thirst to be quenched and a kind soul raised unto Him wine upon a cloth.

Then finally, with a loud cry, Jesus brought His head up to the black sky, speaking the name of His Father, who then called Him forth. I raised my eyes and saw His Great Spirit leave His tired and tortured body as a brilliant Light poured outward and upward from the crown of His head into the Heavens.

From each voice gathered there was released a terrible cry of fear and heartrending pain at the realization that truly this was the Son of God. Seeing now that God, in the form of man, had walked among them, they cried lamentations such as these, "Oh what have we done? What have we done?" Doomed, verily doomed are we!"

The earth did shake as thunder and lightning fell down with the rain, at the moment of His Holy ascension. The fires went out and were lit again by the force of the sky. And the people began to scream again in terror and run toward their homes, as some could be seen already burning in the distance. It was a day and a night like none other, nor will be again.

The faithful, the disciples and I, those who had loved and followed Jesus, even as our hearts were overwhelmed by grief, we also felt a stillness, a peace like no other. We lay on the ground in supplication praying to God, hardly needing the air that we did breathe. It was a peace, beyond understanding, truly beyond the effort of words. The Angels watched over us, knowing, bringing the comfort of God to our hearts. We could not move, we were truly unable, until the man and his servant came forth and took the body of Jesus, the Son of the Highest, down from that cross of pain.

In the quiet darkness, I watched as they brought Him down with great tenderness and reverence. My heart was grieving sorely for my son's death; yet I knew that the world's most terrible loss and greatest gain had begun almost instantly at that moment: when He had released His Holy Spirit unto the Heavens.

Dear reader, even as they lowered Him to the ground, I could not take my eyes off of His wounded feet. Memories of Seeta joyfully washing his feet as an infant, his first steps in Egypt, my mother's kissing them as we came home, running and playing with his dog, Taz, and the many miles of journeys He had walked, bringing the people ever closer to God's eternal love, brought fresh tears to my eyes.

The disciples and the Angels around them lifted me up. They brought me to His body so that I might kiss and hold Him one last time. Oh, His body felt so worn down, so frail, and I knew that He had given to this Earth every single measure of Himself that He could give before this night.

It was not just of great compassion of the Holy Spirit that He died quickly upon the cross, but that He had given His all to this world. There was nothing left. His work was truly done. And ours, his followers, as well as yours and mine, had just begun.

* * *

Late into the night, the disciple, John, who had brought me on the path from Nazareth, then kindly took me to his mother's house where I took Sabbath and slept for many days. My sleep was deep, and yet I had many dreams of my Son and the Holy Host of Angels. I saw in my dreams, visions of Jesus ascending to God in the form of the brightest, yet most peaceful Light, which held the deepest Love that we in the earthly world could barely comprehend.

Comfort was given to my heart, when I saw in my dreams, His Love for the World as He came back to speak to His disciples more than once. I knew then, when I awoke, that He would always be with us, that God's incomprehensible Love, would always be only a prayer, a quiet conversation with Jesus, a heart to heart beat away.

This story, I give to you, dear reader. Please pass it on as a loving mother from my heart. And as Jesus said, "Love one another." It is the greatest commandment. He was the Teacher, the walking, breathing Healer who exemplified that reflection of God's Love for you.

Dear reader, my dearest one, always be vigilant and do not let hate dwell for a moment in your heart. This darkness will never serve you, but only use you, dry you up, and cast you to the winds.

It is Love that will serve you. Love will nourish your heart and all those you love. In This, all of your blessings shall be nourished as well.

This is why Jesus taught forgiveness, that your heart might be set free to Love. That you would have an unbroken connection in God's Heart for you. And those you will forgive shall be freed as well, so that God's Love will surely go on and on in this world and beyond.

God's Peace be with you, my dear one. Always.

Epilogue

After Mary had finished telling her story, I asked if she would perhaps talk about her life after the crucifixion, but she indicated that there was nothing further that she needed to share. My feeling then was, that after Jesus had gone to the Father, she felt that the rest of her time on earth was of little consequence. Not that she died soon after, I am certain that she went back to be with her family, and that John, the disciple whom Jesus specifically asked to watch over Her, was always close by. But it was after her own ascension, that Her Heavenly work began and part of that work is telling Her story. Why? So that it might help you to realize your own ascension to the Light and know the great Love that God has for you. This is Mary's wish for you.

* * *

So now I am honored to share a few of the messages which Mother Mary gave over the years, as I sat before her in meditation. These messages and my ability to receive them seemed to evolve over time as they became more detailed and clear.

Messages from Mother Mary

Here is a vision and a message from one of the first Circles of Mary, in November 2007, which I had written down after everyone left. (Although Mother Mary initially asked that the Circle of Mary be a circle of women, slowly men asked to join in and were sometimes brought in by their partners. All were warmly welcomed by Her).

Tonight, the Circle of Mary met with a great blessing of Mother Mary's presence. We meditated and I felt a strong urgency to channel. I first saw pink roses filling the room, and I felt such Love and deep peace. These words I write cannot describe the feeling of blessing, joy and amazement.

Then, I had a vision of a silver needle with a strong thread, stitching through a tapestry, stitching and gliding, stitching and gliding. Mother Mary was showing me that each step we take, each decision we make, weaves and creates the tapestry, the foundation of our lives.

"We weave the story upon which we stand," She said. "Is our foundation strong, or random and loose? What kind of thread do we use to create our story upon which we stand?"

I thought, *can we go back and strengthen our weaving? Is it possible?* "Yes, she said, "with forgiveness."

"As you create, stitch a strong fabric, then those who are strong, those who have integrity, will choose to stand there with you. However, if your tapestry is loose, full of fear, unkindness and irresponsibility, then only the weak-minded will take a step toward your shaky foundation. Choose wisely then, the steps, the foundation, the tapestry, which you strive to create every day."

After the loving attendants of the Circle of Mary had left and I had written down this message from Mary, I understood that I could receive and write messages from Her in quiet times alone. So, I began to sit with Her from time to time with pen and notebook always at hand.

Sometimes I would ask a question and sometimes just sit in the bliss of Her Presence. At other times, I would only have a passing thought and Her Loving teachings would quickly come through. After writing down each lesson, I found it enriching to sit and absorb the knowledge within my heart. "Sitting still with gratitude of each day's blessing increases its magnitude," Mother Mary told me.

Here are a few of the deepest messages which I have received from Mother Mary over the years:

First, I will let you know that as I was channeling at the beginning of Her story, when She began to talk about, "In a new incarnation, a new life, there is not the time to relive the past. Each lifetime's lessons, each single day is packed full, as you would call it. Even the days when it would seem to you that there is nothing going on, nothing happening. These days are carefully fitted into the lifetime for a reason, for a purpose." I asked this question:

"Mother Mary, my question is, if all of our days are carefully fitted, carefully planned...?" (And She did not let me finish). "You have the gift of Free Will of course," She said. "God is not a taskmaster. Even the days in which you live have been chosen, co-chosen by you. So that the knowing of our lives in the past, for the most part, would only hold us back, would impede the progress."

"What about the stories of people who vividly remember their recent past life?"

"Two things. These are very rare incarnations. These are souls who have reincarnated too quickly and feel they have unfinished business, unfinished processing of the lessons they have learned from the previous lifetime. They are still attached and have a strong need to return in any way they possibly can. This can be seen for them, almost as a time warp situation.

We the Light Beings, the Angels, try to convince them to rest on the heavenly plan, to process their earthly past slowly and deeply before incarnating once again. But they do not wish to listen. So then, it is their choice to reincarnate quickly, their free will.

We are happy to say that these choices are rare, since there is much unhappiness in such a life. Within these souls, there is always the feeling of deep sadness, of not belonging. There is always the question of, 'Why am I here?'

However, the second aspect is this: these souls have also made another choice, to live the difficult life of being a true teacher of reincarnation. Of teaching mankind that we have lived in the past and that our lifetime here is precious and brings with us the knowledge that there is a rich tapestry of wisdom within our beings and not just the here and now. That this life is not just something finite. There is something of ourselves beyond ourselves. There is God's eternal wisdom, His wise and Loving plan for us. And so, these souls are teachers, reminders of this past life experience."

About Predestination and Prayer

"Prayer is the highway, the connection to God. There is predestination. Some things are permanent, unchangeable. Some are not. There is free will, which we will discuss later. Prayer is a powerful force. More powerful than you know. Strong prayer can bend the ear of God, since God is so close. God is within you. Pray from your heart. Go into silence before you pray. Pray for sight and insight. Pray for knowledge of right and wrong. Ask that all personal judgments be removed from the situation you are praying for. Ask for the true connection, (the highway) to God's heart. Feel it and then pray."

On Creating Peace

One evening I sat before Mary just to find peace, being upset about the news of the world when she spoke:

"There could be peace on Earth and it is easy. Take out of the equation greed, which is perpetuated by fear. Fear that God doesn't love me enough, or only I have the reigns of my life and I don't have to think about it. I don't believe in His Love. Therefore, I will take more, I will want more of what another has. Or I will take away what another has to make myself feel better. Such pain! Such suffering is this!

Turn to the Light, to the Unconditional Love of God. That Love, that Peace beyond all understanding. It is always there at hand, right there within you.

Seek and you will find it. Go there peacefully

every day. Set aside the time. No one has to hold your hand. You've got this. You have the reigns of peace-fullness and the Power of Heavenly Love within your Heart Center.

What is the next step? What will be the unfoldment? Listen."

On Judgment and Self-judgment/Criticism

"There is no judgment from Spirit. You only judge yourself. Self-judgment is a stirring within to correct and balance the Life.

But feel the Love, always there from God. Always in the Heart. Always.

This will make the correction, the balance easy.

Then meditate, open to Wisdom and Lovingly make your way into His Arms.

Judging others is not a knowing. It is a self-judging in a harsher form. This is a separation from God. This is why He said, 'Judge not lest ye be judged.'

This Truth is given in the Highest Love."

On Stealing

"Never steal. What belongs to you, belongs to you. If you take from another and claim it as your own, it is not yours. It still belongs to another. It is displaced and not a part of you and disrupts the fabric, the foundation upon which you attempt to stand.

We say attempt, because in stealing, whether it is an object, a body of work, or even a life, one cannot fully stand straight with honor and integrity. One cannot joyfully open the arms and receive the fullness of God's rich blessings of Love.

To receive the blessing of forgiveness, pay back that which you owe in full measure."

Losing Loved Ones

A young woman in our town had died while cycling with some friends. Another woman had lost control of her vehicle and ran into her, killing her almost instantly.

"Dear Mother Mary," I asked, **"I know why people have to die, as this is the cycle of life. But why people so young and full of promise? And when they are taken, why do their friends and families have to suffer so much?"**

"The path a soul walks upon, she does not walk alone. Imagine a person walking down a path and see energy lines. Yes, much like the translucent web lines of a spider coming from that soul walking, striding or running down that path. To each line is a person connected to that soul. Some of the connected ones are leading, some are beside and some are behind the traveler as she walks. Some are close and some are farther away.

When a person dies, all of these lines are severed and the soul is then set free. So then death could be seen as the ultimate freedom, which God has given. Those who experience their connective line to a loved one cut, can feel true pain. For the energy from the shining soul is immense and so that loss of energy, especially when cut quickly, without expectation, is the hardest separation, the deepest wound we know. It is like taking a meal every day and then suddenly, intensely, there is starvation and confusion.

This is why God has given the gift of tears, which help to drown, mute, and wash away the pain. Tears bring release and a binding of the wound of separation. Compassion within the hearts of the connected ones is a gift from God as well. And time."

I continued my question later about tragic deaths:

An earthquake had happened in the world and

many people had died. I sat at the altar in tears and Mother Mary wisely said,

"The time of death is always Planned. We say Planned with a capital P because it is God's Will."

What about group catastrophes when many people die? I thought.

"These people have Collective Karma as you would call it. They come together to experience the same ending. The families and friends who are left behind to grieve – they have a bond in the collective, too. Then, Time and the Holy Spirit come in for the Healing of the emotionally and physically wounded. Tears are water for cleansing. Spring flowers come for the uplifting of the Soul. This is the cycle of Life, which sometimes appears as experiences barely comprehensible for humans. This is why the Angels are sent for comfort and consolation in these times. Look for them."

About Pets

One evening as I sat in front of my altar, my orange tabby cat decided to sit on the altar next to Mary and be worshipped as well, as cats are known to do. I thought, at that moment, how lovely and comforting it was just to have my beloved kitty, Goldie Locks, in the room.

Then Mary spoke, "Knowing that humans, who are of the flesh, need to feel that physical presence of Unconditional Love, God the Grace of Pure Love, did send these beings to comfort and uplift the heart. Know them as a treasured Gift from God."

* * *

After the last of the seven messages to the Circle of Mary in 2007, Mary sent a physical confirmation of Her presence and her messages. I feel Her Presence now and know that She would like to have it included here.

Mother Mary and Her Crop Circle

Dear Circle of Mary Sisters,

So, the seven Sundays of the Circle of Mary have ended. It feels like a completion, but also a start. I wanted to let you know about a phenomenon which happened in the form of a crop circle. People have asked me if I know whether crop circles are real or not. My answer is yes, most crop circles are real and not made by humans. Some, however, are made by people in an attempt to duplicate them. However, most crop circles are so complex, beautiful and large, and reportedly are formed in a very short amount of time. They just could not be "human made."

Circle Sisters, some of you know I had an incredible experience and message from Christ while I was in England in 2006. At that time, I prayed to be shown a crop circle to affirm His message was the truth. Then the crop circle showing the two hearts and a star appeared in Wiltshire the next day!

You can see the message which Jesus gave, as well as the photos of the apparition at the Chalice Well at this site: www.iriseabove.com/apparition.html.

Naturally, as these seven messages from Mary were channeled, I thought it would be interesting if a crop circle for the Circle of Mary might appear. This was just a passing thought and not even a prayer request. A few days later, I checked the very informative crop circle website: www.temporarytemples.co.uk and indeed it had come! On July 25th, 2007 a crop circle formation, at West Kennett Longbarrow, Wiltshire, showing the feminine symbol, a star within and circle above had appeared.

I am attaching a photo from the site of the crop circle for you to see. Thank you, Circle of Mary sisters, for your support and I know Mother Mary does, too. I encourage you all to go back and read these messages again. Send Love to all the world and also grow from the meditations which were given, and of course, help others to find peace and healing, too. It is from helping others that we also are uplifted and continue to grow.

> With Unconditional Love,
> Mother Mary and Rev. Elizabeth Alder

* * *

The photograph of the apparition of Christ at the Chalice Well came about when I went on a tour to the British Isles with my friend and beloved spiritual woman, Christy Gray. This was just before the advent of digital cameras, at least in my world, in 2006. Christy had loaned me her camera for the trip, so of course, I took as many photos as I could of England's glorious countryside. When we visited the Chalice Well Gardens in Glastonbury, I knelt down before the Lion's Head Fountain.

As I was getting ready to take a picture, I thought about a vision I had had when I was just 23 years old. I was meditating and I had heard George Harrison's song, "My Sweet Lord," that morning. The famous George Harrison of the Beatles, was singing a song of wanting to be so close to God that he could see Him.

So, with my eyes closed in meditation, I thought, *How can I see You in this lifetime Lord? I am sure it will take many, many years*. At that moment, the most beautiful and happiest smile you can imagine appeared and I burst out laughing in joy and wonder of what this could be. Then I realized it was the Christ himself! I fell over, trying to catch my breath, laughing and crying all at once. This is what I was thinking about as I was preparing to take the picture.

After I arrived back home in the United States and had the pictures developed, I saw in the picture I had taken at the Chalice Well, the apparition of Christ. Almost disbelieving, I cried, as I stared at this miracle for what seemed like an eternity. How could this be?

The next day, I showed the photo to a friend, without telling her anything about it. She was a Baptist minister's wife and said immediately, "Oh! There's Jesus!" A confirmation from a strong source.

A year later, I went back to England and received a message from Christ on the second night I was there. Later that week, I took the picture and the written message to the office at the Chalice Well Garden; they encouraged me to make bookmarks with the picture on the front and the message on the back. I am ever grateful for their wise guidance.

This is the message Jesus gave that night in England:

The second night in England I could not sleep, though I was so very tired. I kept seeing a vision of someone's feet standing in the waters of the Lion's Head Fountain at the Chalice Well Garden. Each time, as I was trying to get comfortable, I prayed to God, "Oh, please let me get some sleep! Why are you showing me this?" But the vision only became bigger and bigger, until it became as big as a movie screen and was not to be denied.

At that moment, I realized what I had been shown all through the night. These were the feet of Christ! Jesus, was standing in the waters of the Chalice Well, His wounds bleeding, turning the water a deep red. At daybreak, compassion came and I said, "Oh, I am so sorry for your pain. This must really hurt you!"

Then He spoke, "Yes, I am very hurt. I am hurt because people are fighting in my name and in the name of religion. This is not what I want. "What do you want Lord?" I asked. Then Jesus said, "I want people to love themselves so deeply, so sweetly, that it spills over for the Love of Humanity. This is the true Love of God. In this, the Peace, the Healing begins. Later that day, as I was touring the countryside, I looked up at a cross atop a little church and another message from the Lord came to me. "Beloved, I want people to put down the cross."

"Why Lord?" I asked, confused at such a statement from Him. "The cross is a symbol of torture, pain and oppression. I do not wish this to be my symbol any longer. When I was a newborn baby, my first symbol was a Star, high in the heavens. This is the True Image of God, the Glory and the Light. I want people to rise above and be the Star that they are. The cross is man-made and the Star is God made."

This is Mary's story, which She lovingly gives to you as her humble gift. Know that Mary's comforting presence is always there whenever you need Her. Mother Mary's heart is always open to you. Envision Her Loving Arms around you whenever you feel alone, afraid, or just need deep, abiding peace at that moment in your life. As Her Beloved Son said, "Ask and you shall receive."

I am honored and so humbled to bring Mary's story to you. I hope you will share Her wisdom with others, for as She said in the beginning, "I urge you to let me speak to the world."

Gratefully,
Rev. Elizabeth Grace Alder

Acknowledgments

First and foremost! Blessings of love and a deep thank you to all the writers before and after me, who have taken the leap to listen to and write down the words which Loving Spirits have whispered into their hearts.

Thank you as well to:

Mark Katzman and participants of the Hargrett's Writers Circle, whose encouragement first led me to bring Mother Mary's story into book form.

Lisa Smartt, whose generosity, bright energy and amazing knowledge of writing helped me to navigate the book writing path and to connect me with so many who have helped bring this work together.

Dr. Raymond Moody, a pioneer through his research and writing of near-death experiences, who has given so much to humanity. Helping all of us know that we are much more than just finite human beings, but infinite and enriching souls with a purpose of love in this world and beyond.

A big thank you to my editor, Jill Hartmann-Roberts, for her sweet and infinite patience.

A heartfelt thank you to Katherine Cerulean, for her work in bringing Mary's story into book form.

Thank you as well to my loving friends and family. And especially, my late stepfather and hero, Harvey Joseph Cohen, who taught me laughter, generosity and integrity, which I have carried in my heart throughout my life.

Made in the USA
Monee, IL
13 February 2020

21528550R00090